— G O D —
Has No Blind Alleys

— GOD —
Has No Blind Alleys

A Memoir by RON MILLSON

iUniverse LLC
Bloomington

GOD HAS NO BLIND ALLEYS

iUniverse books may be ordered through booksellers or by contacting:

iUniverse
1663 Liberty Drive
Bloomington, IN 47403
www.iuniverse.com
1-800-Authors (1-800-288-4677)

Because of the dynamic nature of the Internet, any web addresses or links contained in this book may have changed since publication and may no longer be valid. The views expressed in this work are solely those of the author and do not necessarily reflect the views of the publisher, and the publisher hereby disclaims any responsibility for them.

Certain stock imagery © Thinkstock.
Any people depicted in stock imagery provided by Thinkstock are models, and such images are being used for illustrative purposes only.

All Scripture quotations are taken from the *New King James Version*. Copyright © 1989 by Thomas Nelson, Inc. Used by permission. All rights reserved.

ISBN: 978-1-4917-3383-7 (e)
ISBN: 978-1-4917-3384-4 (sc)

Library of Congress Control Number: 2014908100

Printed in the United States of America.

iUniverse rev. date: 6/6/2014

This book is dedicated to my beloved wife and co-worker, Verna. Without her labours, this achievement never could have been brought into existence. It is also dedicated to our children Susan, Stephen, Lyn and Mary, and to our grandchildren and great-grandchildren.

CONTENTS

LIST OF ILLUSTRATIONS

PREFACE

Now that school was out for the year, all the examinations were written, and I was free at last from the humdrum of concentrating on textbooks, the first thing on my mind was escaping the heat of the first days of summer. Some of my chums, also affected by the temperature, had similar thoughts of the swimming hole, our favourite place to go when the heat was depressing us. We called the road where that special place of refreshment was located the "Blind Fourth." It was a strange name for a road, but we called it that because, according to the road map, it was the fourth main concession road northeast of the city of London, Ontario, where I lived in my early years. Furthermore, folks who lived in that area knew that road went nowhere except to a river where there was a good place to swim. If a stranger were to travel in the area and turned his car in that direction, he would soon find out that the road was a blind alley. But even a blind alley can hold surprises at its end. It can be refreshing and satisfying to dive in and experience whatever is on offer. I'm sure everyone can visualize the simple pleasure illustrated by the preceding anecdote. A cool swim on a hot day is truly refreshing. But there is another side to the blind alley metaphor: Imagine you are a motorist with social plans. You want to arrive at your destination without stopping along the way. In this case, running into a blind alley could be frustrating.

God creates blind alleys in the lives of His servants for different purposes. It may be that you need to stop and rest a while, or it may be that you must wait for other circumstances in your life to work out. In such a case, what seems to be a blind alley could, in reality, be a necessary pause in your program until things are lined up for you to forge ahead. Or perhaps you need a fresh view of God in order to prepare for what He has planned ahead for you.

Christians need to understand the truth that is stated in the title of this book: God has no blind alleys. He leads and guides His servants, so things will always work out; God is unstoppable. "All the inhabitants of the earth are reputed as nothing; He does *according to His will* in the army of heaven and among the inhabitants of the earth. No one can restrain his hand or say to Him, 'What have you done?'" (Daniel 5:35, italics mine). God knows what He is doing and how He wants it done. Blessed are those whom He has chosen to serve Him in accomplishing His will.

As we continue this narrative, you will read about how my wife and I anticipated an exciting experience serving God but were filled with disappointment and confusion. Until, that is, we learned through one of His servants that God has no blind alleys. Rather, they are pathways of joy, pleasure and refreshment in seeing His will fulfilled in our lives. Read on and you will see what God can do when we do not stand in his way but obediently follow.

—————— ACKNOWLEDGEMENTS ——————

I am grateful for the support and understanding of my dear wife, Verna, who patiently endured my absences and hibernation in my study to recall the events of those early days realizing the dream of Wildwood Bible Camp.

My thanks and appreciation also go to my dear friend and brother in Christ, Arnold Spears, who offered profitable suggestions and advice when I leaned upon his experience as a secondary-school English teacher. In recent years, we have enjoyed the setting of Wildwood as a place of retreat to study the Scriptures together.

My thanks go to Jim Demers, our helpful neighbour, who suggested that *Wildwood* might be a good name for the camp. I thought it seemed fitting, and it was.

Last, but not least, I am thankful to the living and personal God of all Christians who, by His grace, granted us the faith to believe that all things we needed and hoped for would be supplied without solicitation. Our confidence in this is in Hebrews 11:1, "Now faith is the substance of things hoped for, the evidence of things not seen."

As well, I am thankful to Him for enabling me to recall from my memory banks the many details I have recorded here. As I mentioned previously, this narrative is accurate in all of its general details. I wish to give worthy recognition to all of you who laboured with us over the years, but unfortunately, many names have been left out—not on purpose, but due to my inability to recall details of your labours of love and your names. In the future, the God whom you were serving will generously offer you His thanks and His reward.

INTRODUCTION

The theme and title of this book may be of little interest to the average person, but it may serve as a strong message of encouragement to those who feel they are at a blind alley and do not know what to do. I would be gratified for my experience to prove helpful to others who are longing to be actively used by God. As you will read in this book, I myself was in this very circumstance and believed I had lost my way. I had made extreme changes of profession and residence that affected my family and the security of our future in order to answer a call that I was convinced was from well-meaning people and from God. And yet, upon moving to the new area, reality subdued me with discouragement. I felt I was at an end of a road that was going nowhere: a blind alley. However, I became so engrossed in attending to our present needs that the primary issue of why we were there became a secondary one that lost its nagging and discouraging influence. I learned that waiting on God was one of the first lessons in following Him. If you wholeheartedly want to serve Him, learn to wait on *God's* timing. It will save you hours of wasted effort forging ahead without His guidance. What to you seems like a blind alley may not be one at all.

Our blind-alley problem had to do with a request to provide leadership in the creation of a Christian camp in northern Ontario.

I felt I was qualified, as did the others who wanted us. My first camp experience came when I was 30 years old. I had never before known that such a place as a Christian camp existed. Because of my age, I was approached by responsible people who asked me to be a counsellor at Forest Cliff Boys Camp. I asked innocently, "But how will I fit in? I have no experience." They described to me what was expected of a counsellor in that context. The main thing was to live as an example of what a Christian should be and to give guidance and direction to young boys. Besides this, I should do my part in supporting the main program of giving the campers a good time. Since it was a Christian camp, I was wisely advised to give the boys not-too-pushy direction about the need to receive Jesus Christ as Saviour and Lord of their lives. These were the essentials. Gladly, yet with caution, I assented to come. The month passed by quickly and I enjoyed every minute of it. I counselled at the camp for four years, during which I was made the director of the whole camp program. This was a new adventure. In truth, when the appointment was offered to me, I accepted it with fearfulness.

I had no idea how to organize or direct the entire program. This involved two boys' camps of approximately 120 boys each and the responsibility of assigning the many counsellors to suitable cabins and age groups. I also had to organize the sports program and the Bible study periods, assigning capable instructors who could suitably tend the spiritual needs of the children. At the end of the summer I was weary, but I was still surviving.

This experience, helped to set the course for the years that followed. The persuasive value of Christian camping was on my heart for some time, so I offered to become the full-time director of the camp, working year-round. However, the Board of Trustees was not in a position to employ anyone in a full-time capacity, so my offer was declined. Still, my interest in camping persisted and I thought about it now and again at different times. This interest stirred me to seriously consider the request that was to come from another source.

The folks in Chapleau wanted us to return to help start up a camp. My wife and I were immediately interested and made major changes in our lives so we could work on this project. But upon moving to the new location, what we found disappointed and depressed us. We became confused and didn't know what to do. What follows is the story of how the whole incident revolutionized our Christian lives by teaching us that God does not lead us into blind alleys. Rather, He leads us into circumstances in which we learn principles for following Him and we see Him open doors that we have no power to open. The writer of the Proverb 3:6 says, "In all your ways acknowledge Him and He shall direct your paths."

CHAPTER 1

Preparatory Years

A Like-minded Partner

When I was a child of 12, I spent my summers on my grandfather's farm. He had been a widower for a few years, and my mother sent me there to keep him company, and to keep me off the streets, where I might get into trouble. Occasionally, my grandfather would harness up his brown mare to the buggy and then trot away to visit his friend Billy Dawson just a couple of miles away. They went to the same church and were good friends. I would be left alone, my eyes following him until he was out of sight.

In my younger years, I was unaware of the Lord's preparations in my life in regard to what would follow. I was farming near London, Ontario, engrossed in what that occupation demands. Yet I knew there was something more to life than what I had at the time. In those early days, I was caring for my aging parents and enriching my life through reading. This led me to read about how the Gospels offered forgiveness of sins through faith in the Lord Jesus Christ. I believed and became a born-again Christian. I was 21 at the time and convinced this was the *something* I had been missing in life. Immediately, my interests turned to spiritual things. Soon after, I was led to attend a young people's meeting at a Baptist church. There, a girl caught my attention. She had been invited there to sing a couple of Christian songs by the teacher leading the gathering. While she was singing, a thought crossed my mind: *What if I came to know her well and married her?* At the invitation of the teacher, the girl, who was named Verna, began attending the group as well.

After some weeks, Verna invited me to her house, which was not far from the church. Her mother asked me questions about my parents and their background, and we discovered that my mother had gone to the same church she attended years ago. In conversation, she mentioned that her maiden name was Lily Dawson. In surprise, I realized that she was the daughter of Billy Dawson, my grandfather's friend, and Verna was his granddaughter. Sometimes I wonder what my grandfather, if he were living today, would say about my having married the granddaughter of his friend. It would probably be something like "Humph." Then he would smile, light up his pipe and sport a broad grin of approval. I had seen him do this many times when I was 12 years old. As the weeks went by, I spent more and more time in Verna's company and at their home.

Soon after, I enrolled in the Pastor's Course at London Bible College. At first, my aim was to keep farming while I attended school. Common sense soon told me that I couldn't do both. I spoke to my parents about my new views on life, my keen interest in studying the Bible and my desire to make this my life's profession. Their attitude was sympathetic and understanding, so I sold my farm machinery and livestock, and we moved to London. This proved to be a better environment for my parents too, due to their advanced years.

Since we no longer had the farm and the meagre income it provided, I had to secure a job. I found one with Kellogg Canada, working on the night shift. This allowed me to attend classes at London Bible College from 8:30 a.m. until 12:30 p.m., do my class assignments and catch some sleep before going to work from 11:00 p.m. to 7:00 a.m.. Though I was young and took time for the occasional diversion from my tight schedule, I found it was too much for me. It was not long before my health began to fail. After three years of school, I had to leave college just prior to graduation. However, I had gained Bible knowledge, and most importantly, knowledge of proper Christian doctrine, biblical terminology and the principles of Bible study. Because I had not completed my course, I could not pursue a pastorate in a church, but I had become acquainted with how the brethren view the Scriptures; I associated myself with that fellowship.

After leaving Bible College, I sought secular employment somewhere other than Kellogg. I found this in carpentry work in the city of London, Ontario. This work mainly involved building houses, from the concrete footings to the ridge of the roof. One day I was given the choice of either joining the union or losing my job. As a Christian, I knew joining the union meant sharing an unequal yoke with unbelievers. This would never work out due to my convictions, since it went against Christian principles as seen in the New Testament. If it came to the matter of a strike, according to Christian principles, I could not stand with them. Consequently, I approached the superintendent of the subdivision in which I was working and tendered my resignation, explaining my convictions. He quickly replied, "That is no problem. Why don't you become an independent contractor, and I will give you all the roofing in this subdivision and in others." I immediately did as he suggested. I also needed a partner, and I found one in my good friend and brother in Christ, Ernest Sanders.

Ernie and I were close friends, and he was a groomsman at my wedding to Verna Harris in June 1954. Ernie and I worked together as roofers and expanded into insulating and installing plasterboard in houses and then into building houses and performing other renovations. This business lasted for four years, until Ernie felt called to become a schoolteacher. Naturally gifted in teaching, he continued on in this direction. Rather than be left to myself, climbing all over roofs, I decided to improve my education too. I entered a local teachers' college in London, and after one year I graduated as a fully licensed public-school teacher.

After teaching for two years, I was asked to teach in the north of Ontario, where we could help in a fledgling Christian community. This was in 1960. Verna and I were in Chapleau for three years and became warmly engaged working with the Christian fellowship there. To illustrate what the terrain and isolation of parts of the north are like, I include the following experience that Verna and I had within our first year there.

During the spring break, we decided to go on a little holiday. In the northern part of the province, it can be cold, but invigorating. Susan, our first child, had been born about four months ago, so we decided to return south to London to allow our family and friends to meet her. My wife has a generous heart; she had previously invited a friend in town, an elderly woman, to go to London with us to visit some friends that she knew. She had gladly accepted and was with us now on our return trip. Verna insisted our friend sit in the front seat beside me, since it would be more comfortable.

It was late in the afternoon, and the sun was nearing the horizon. The road was gravelly, very rough and deeply rutted by heavy truckloads of lumber journeying to the big cities farther south. The roads had frozen during the winter. Now the pleasant warmth of spring had returned to thaw out the roads, making them difficult to traverse. The traffic was negligible, in part because of the road conditions. We were about 75 miles from our destination.

At about 4:30 p.m., our '51 Plymouth began to labour and then to slow down. I glanced at the gauges and saw, to my surprise, that the temperature was as high as it could register. I stopped the car, lifted the hood and was dismayed to discover the fan belt had broken. I felt slightly panicked because I knew we were in serious trouble. There was no place to go for help for miles in that area. To make matters more tense, our infant child was crying to be fed, now reminding me she was on board too. Verna had been hoping to stop for at least a few minutes so we could put Susan's bottle on the car engine to warm it for her. Her wish had come true, but my wish was for another fan belt! We were faced with two urgent problems: a crying baby needing to be fed and the need for a fan belt. The latter was the most urgent in my mind since it was getting darker by the minute and would soon be much colder. However, warming the baby's bottle on the hot car engine came first.

I stood by the car for a moment and raised a prayer to God for wisdom. My Christian faith was being put to the test. Considering the difficulty we were in, I asked God for some direction about what to do. Immediately, a verse of Scripture came to mind: "What is that in thine hand?"(Exodus 4:2). Looking at my hands, I saw, of course, nothing there. After a few moments, I thought, *You dumb bunny, could the Lord mean "What have you got with you?"* I looked inside the car trunk and found an old canvas with tie-down ropes on it. About a year earlier, I had put it in there, thinking, *Someday, I may have need of it.* That day was now.

I have found that, for any difficulty we might face, the Lord will generally have led us to do something earlier in preparation for it. Or He may lead us to make some provision to meet a specific need we might face in future. This is because, in all things, He knows the end from the beginning (Isaiah 46:10). In this case, our provision was in the trunk of the car.

In my early teens, summers had been spent on my uncle's farm working, watching and helping him do mechanical repairs. This was how I had gained the advantage and the ability to repair many types of broken machinery, including knowing how to splice a rope when the hayfork rope broke due to excessive wear. This occasionally happened during haying time. I had my penknife with me; I quickly cut the ropes from the canvas. Since they were only a quarter of an inch in diameter, I wished they were heavier. This cast the shadow of doubt into my mind; I was concerned about whether they would be strong enough to get us home. Still, I proceeded to splice them together, doing what I had seen my uncle do. I connected them, making a continuous rope that would serve as a fan belt. Then, with some difficulty, I squeezed it over the pulleys.

My hands grew quite cold while I worked on the splice in the chilly air. When I got back into the car, which was still a comfortable temperature, I mentioned that my hands were cold. Mrs. Collings, who had a motherly heart, said, "Here, let me warm them for you." I had not assented, but she reached over, took my two hands and proceeded to warm them by holding them *very* tightly in hers. My hands had become numb, and when she did this, the pain nearly sent me through the roof! Striving to be gentlemanly, I said nothing and endured it. I can still remember this event as if it were yesterday.

We headed for home. After about five or six miles, I noticed the temperature gauge indicated the car was heating up again. I stopped again and discovered that the problem was simple: the rope fan belt was too loose and was slipping. I simply shortened it, and we were on our way again. The anxiety of the moment soon left me and our car conversation continued. This impromptu fan belt did the job so well that it got us all the way home. In fact, I didn't even get a proper new fan belt until about a month later.

We lived in that area for three years before moving back to southern Ontario, where we settled to teach around Guelph. I spent four years in that position, and then came the project which is the subject of this book. We had a visit from the folks in Chapleau asking us to return. To fulfill this request, it would be necessary to start a new phase of our Christian life. We eventually saw that this had been the reason for our move to Guelph. I will explain this further in subsequent chapters.

A Work of Man or of God?

The establishment of this Christian camp which people now enjoy was entirely a work of the Lord and of His provisions. The New Testament is clear: When a Christian does any service for God, he must be led by the Holy Spirit and follow the direction the Spirit gives in doing that work. Otherwise, it is a work of man and will have no lasting value that God can recognize. The Christian knows that God leads in all that is done. This is why we can say confidently that God has no blind alleys; all things will work out and are profitable. If this working with God and seeing lasting results goes on for years, then it is a sacred experience, and we know the work will endure. Many have had the personal experience of being introduced to Jesus Christ in a personal way while at the camp. Others have had the satisfying joy of learning more from the Word of God as it was taught to them by competent instructors. One of these instructors was Dr. Ross Woodward. His teaching clearly pointed to the necessity of a personal relationship with Jesus Christ. Ross and Thelma, his wife, were pitching in with us as usual, sharing the load. He also laboured in other ways such as painting and cleaning up the grounds. We were standing in front of one of the cabins when he asked me a question. He seemed to want to get something settled in his mind. "Is Wildwood Bible Camp something for Ron Millson, or is it the Lord's?" he asked. I responded, "It is the Lord's; we are but servants." At that time, we had all just emerged on the other side of a trial that might have terminated our vision of a Christian camp, the details of which are forthcoming in another chapter. I pondered what had prompted Dr. Woodward to ask this question and concluded that he may have been wondering who was behind the camp and who had started it. He may have thought, "Millson seems to be the only one in authority and leadership here. Who else is involved?" These are only assumptions on my part, but these questions are logical and fair ones.

The camp had no board of directors at the time. The board members had all left due to job transfer, or disinterest, or, in one case, due to personal conflict with another board member. As a result, we had to establish the camp by our own by physical labour, or else it would not have existed at all. It looked as if I was doing all the work myself and the camp was mine; this was not the case. In reality, I was in the process of establishing another board to provide the camp with a proper authority. But board members had to be first proven in different ways before they would be asked to take the position, and that took time.

LIKE-MINDED PEOPLE

Those involved in this project were only God's servants, since all of the labour and financial gifts received were given unto the Lord and for the Lord's work. This participation was a reflection of people's gratitude and dedication to our loving God and Father in heaven. He is a caring God; He so loved the world that He gave His only begotten Son to redeem us and to bring us into His family. The world needs to know this precious truth. Those who laboured with us were of one mind in this. God delights when we love and trust in Him and direct our faith toward Him. "Without faith it is impossible to please Him, for he that comes to God must believe that He is, and that He is a rewarder of those who diligently seek Him" (Hebrews 11:6).

About this time, I had been studying in the Bible the topic of fellowship. The apostle Paul used this word when he wrote to the young church in Corinth at the beginning of his first letter to them, namely 1 Corinthians 1:9. Those who are called into the fellowship of His Son, Jesus Christ our Lord, and respond to that invitation, are highly privileged and richly blessed. Key to the meaning of this word in the original Greek text is the idea of partnership. As well, note that those within the fellowship will find God faithful. In other words, He will be faithful in His role in that partnership, and He expects us to be steadfast as well. This is only reasonable. It is also a truth all Christians needed to know.

Fellowship manifests as the fundamental principle of togetherness, a relationship which is expressed by all members of the Body of Christ working together in submission to the Head, which is Jesus Christ, our Lord, and under the guidance of the Holy Spirit of God. Since Christ is the Head of His body (the

Church), we must receive our instructions from Him and, whatever we are convinced is His will, act in unity with His Lordship and direction. We must always work with the view of keeping harmony within the body (the Church). This concept is enlarged in 1 John 1:3: "Our fellowship [partnership] is with the Father and with His Son Jesus Christ." Not included here but understood is that the fellowship (or partnership) includes the Holy Spirit, who indwells and empowers the believers with the love and joy of God.

Like-minded Convictions

The intent of the camp ministry from the beginning was to preach the good news of God's love, giving to all who came the opportunity to know the way of salvation and the love of God through His Son Jesus Christ. Also, all who have that knowledge may hunger to hear more of God's ways, to grow in grace and to become followers of the Lord. This concept has been referred to earlier, but it is worthy of repetition.

The work was of God because it was anticipated and begun without any cash on hand, or resources, or assurance from humans, or loans from financial institutions. Nor was there any encouragement, financially or otherwise, from any Christian assembly who may have been aware of what we were doing. In later times, there were contributions, but not at the beginning. This camp was a faith work from the beginning and, during my time as administrator, it continued as such. We looked to the Lord for the supply of materials and financial provision to pay the bills. He alone would move the hearts of people to want to contribute financially or otherwise. Nothing was purchased unless we had the assurance that the financial resources were on hand or that they would be.

God continually supplied our needs for the camp, so we knew that He was pleased with what we were doing. We were assured that we were in fellowship with Him in all of those efforts and free of any headaches relative to it as well.

Furthermore, in the faithfulness of the Lord, we were never stopped in our labours due to lack of finances or lack of dedicated workers who came to help lighten the load. The reason? God has no blind alleys. Praise God for the sweet fellowship we had serving and working together! Since there was no solicitation of funds, nor foreseeable provision in the future, we were entirely dependent on the Lord to reveal to us His will, step by step. In this way, we were assured of His presence and had inner peace knowing that what we were doing was of the Lord. I assume the same principles continue today. I have particularly stressed these matters to glorify the Lord, and to emphasize the truth of a well-known statement uttered by Hudson Taylor of the China Inland Mission: "God's work done in God's way will never lack God's supply." Our motive and plan was to do God's work in God's way. It was not my plan to write this book, but it is an answer to the question "How was Wildwood Bible Camp started?" It was started by prayer and waiting on Him for His direction and His supply to carry that direction into reality.

CHAPTER 2

The Awaited Call

You Are Wanted at the Door

In 1966, a series of events took place that eventually led to a major change in our lives. I was in the midst of my seventh year as a public-school teacher in Rockwood, Ontario. One day, in the middle of a lesson, there was a knock at my classroom door. As was our custom, a student answered it, then he turned and said, "Mr. Millson, you are wanted at the door." To my surprise, it was my friend Len Fex from Chapleau. Len was a full-time worker in the service of the Lord, and he had been for several years. After a short greeting, he asked if we would return to Chapleau to give leadership in developing a Christian camp for children and adults. The request startled me at the time, but as I gave it some thought, it stirred a positive challenge within my spirit from which I could not get rest. As mentioned earlier, for the past four years, I had been the director of Forest Cliff Camp during summer vacations. This was just outside of Forest, Ontario. I was sold on Christian camping and its values, and I had previously offered myself as full-time director at that camp, so these matters of camp ministry were very much in my thoughts. When Len announced what was on his mind, a question popped into my mind: *Is the Lord turning us northward again?* As I mused on this, a warm and peaceful refreshment enveloped my emotions.

Len and I chatted briefly about what this would involve, and then we parted, with me giving him assurance that Verna and I would pray about it and let him know when we had some definite direction. I told him that, in order to return to Chapleau for such an undertaking, I felt it would be necessary to be commended to the Lord's work in a formal way. I would have to leave my profession as a schoolteacher and to enter a life by faith regarding financial support. Shortly afterward, we received a letter on behalf of the assembly in Chapleau making the same request. This was to assure us that it was the mind of everyone in fellowship behind Len's request; they wanted us there to help them start a Christian camp. This letter prompted warm thoughts within my heart once more.

I knew the creation of the camp would involve major tasks and many diverse abilities, including

(a) Constant observation regarding preventative maintenance and knowledge of how to perform fix-it jobs as they arose. These are the primary focuses of a farmer in order to save him time and expense. In this I had had much experience.

(b) Mechanical work such as major repairs to keep machinery working. I had gained much experience of mechanics in my early teens while working with my uncle on his farm.

(c) Major carpentry work such as erecting buildings, and masonry work such as building foundations, bricklaying and roofing. I had done all of these things in my twenties while working for a builder in London.

(d) Ability to study Scripture and compose sermons. I had learned how to do this in my three years at Bible college.

(e) Confidence in speaking before an audience and the ability to think on one's feet. These were qualities I had obtained by teaching children at public school for seven years.

We may not be aware of it at the time, but past experience is very helpful in making life choices about where the Lord would have us serve Him. I believe it is God who leads us to make certain choices or to follow certain directions. Assuming that we want to please the Lord in everything we do, the Bible says, "The steps of a good man are ordered by the Lord, and He delights in His way. Though he falls, he shall not be utterly cast down; for the Lord upholds him with His hand" (Psalm 37:23–24). In these five ways, I had been prepared with experience for challenges I would face in the future.

You Are Wanted in Chapleau

That same year that we were invited to return to Chapleau, a well-known couple from the assembly visited us where we lived in

Rockwood to assure us that they meant business about the camp. And during the Christmas break of that school year, 1966–67, I attended the first conference of Literature Crusades in Chicago at Wheaton College. During that event, at least three separate individuals asked if I had ever given thought to returning to Chapleau. There was never any reason offered for their asking of the question. At this point, I was convinced the Lord was directing us again in that direction. To settle my mind about the matter, during the next spring break, I travelled there to attend a meeting of the Wildwood Camp Board.

There was much discussion regarding the pros and cons of the camp, especially about the amount of work involved in bringing it into being. During this first meeting, on a Friday evening, the subject came up of how much to charge for the camping fee. I persuaded the others that the fee should be minimal. One other prominent member wanted to charge nothing at all. This discussion went on for some time; finally, we decided it would be best to adjourn for the night, sleep on it and then possibly make a decision in the morning.

That night, the Chairman had sensed that one Board member was continually in conflict with me during discussions. To everyone's shock, the next morning, he asked that member to resign from the Board. This startling moment registered to me that the chairman was positively behind the idea of the camp and believed nothing should stand in its way. Everyone was disturbed by his decision, including myself. Abruptly, the board member got up and left. The meeting continued throughout the day, but in a considerable state of unrest. However, a decision was reached to look for a campsite. When the meeting was over, I returned to southern Ontario to make plans for moving to Chapleau.

You Are Wanted to Express Agreement

One other member of the Board, along with his wife, did some searching on their own for a suitable site. Shortly after, we received notice from Chapleau that a proposed campsite had been found and that I should return to see it. They all were in agreement that I should give my approval before application was made to the Ministry of Lands and Forests to rent it. As soon as I could, I returned to Chapleau by train.

Four other men and I visited the site. We stepped out of the tangled underbrush and tall evergreens to the sandy shore of placid Lake Hoey. With a broad grin on his face, one of the party said, "This is it, just as Gerry described it: a southern exposure with lots of sunshine, close to the highway, yet far enough away to be quiet." Another piped up, "Most important of all, it's only 22 miles from Chapleau." Most of the men lived in that railroad town and would be making many trips in the interests of the proposed camp in the future. It seemed everyone was in agreement, including me, but we briefly discussed the pros and cons of the site further. After we had made sure we were all satisfied, we sensed the peace that God had given. We all believed that this was the site we should choose. Another brother then suggested we should give thanks for the Lord's leading. Another added, "And also for further guidance from here on." This we did with joy in our hearts. As we anticipated a future Christian camp on this site and retraced our steps back to the highway, we tossed visions of the future camp for children and their families back and forth among us. It was quite obvious that all were exited, visualizing the days ahead.

Soon, a visit was made to what was known in those days as "Lands and Forests," a provincial government office located in

Chapleau. As I recall, nothing stood in the way of our obtaining 365 meters of lake frontage with a 21-year lease. Upon further questioning, we also learned that the property could be purchased for $3500. This was good news and created a real mood of thankfulness and joy among us. One specification required that the property had to be delineated from the rest of the crown land by an authentic survey at our expense. We all agreed to this and a survey was completed in the early fall of 1967, after Verna and I had moved from Rockwood. Eventually, the camp was officially incorporated and named "Wildwood Bible Camp."

You Are Wanted by the Lord

One of the requirements for me to take a leadership position in relation to the camp was that I be commended to Christian ministry as a servant of the Lord. I could see this would be necessary so that I would feel free to set my heart and mind completely on the task before me. Since I had had considerable experience in directing boys' camps, I was expected to give leadership in developing these proposed campgrounds. Thus it was necessary for me to arrange a meeting with the brethren of Guelph Bible Chapel, where Verna and I were in fellowship. I set before the brethren the series of events that led to the decision to start a children and adults' Bible camp in the north, with myself intimately involved in it. I then requested that they send Verna and me forth to serve the Lord in northern Ontario primarily for this purpose and wherever else the Lord may lead. Their reply was that they would consider it, pray about it and let me know at a later date. They did as they said, and all agreed that the Lord wanted us in His Work. In May 1967, we were commended to the Lord's work in northern Ontario. This meant that I had to get into action to organize our move north as soon as possible. Our house had to be sold, my resignation as a teacher had to be submitted and, in their proper order, other ties had to be severed.

You Will Want This to Move

Prior to the matter of commendation, I had been up north by train to give my approval of the campsite. While there, one of the men on the Board had had the insight that I would need a pickup truck at the site to haul lumber and materials. He obtained a good used truck locally and donated it to the Camp for that purpose. He also stated that I was free to use it for my own needs, including for moving our belongings to Chapleau, so I had driven the truck back to southern Ontario instead of taking the train. This proved to be a real blessing from the Lord and it was put to good use. It was the first of many pieces of large equipment needed to do the job that lay ahead.

Most equipment was donated by other Christians or was bought at prices so low they were beyond imagining. To me, these provisions were reminiscent of how the Lord had fed the millions of the children of Israel as He led them through the wilderness. We were trusting the Lord for everything, even our daily bread. How precious was our fellowship with our heavenly Father in providing all of our needs! We were conscious in our faith that God does not lead us up any blind alleys, although this was yet to be challenged.

It wasn't long before business was settled in Rockwood, all ties were cut in southern Ontario and we were on our way to Chapleau. Verna and I looked forward to our days there with our two children,

Susan, 6, and Stephen, 4. Our house had been sold and all the bills were paid with $5000 clear to start anew in the town of Chapleau. We knew the days ahead involved living by faith from day to day as we had no foreseeable income in the future. But we had perfect peace that God, who is faithful, would take care of us.

CHAPTER 3

Uncertain Waters

Walking on the Water

As I look back, I sometimes wonder what some people may have thought about what Verna and I did. We had left behind everything: home, profession, security and contentment. Besides that, we had virtually no heavy tools or equipment with which to work other than a few carpentry tools and a little eight-inch table saw. Thankfully, we also had the half-ton GMC truck which, as I mentioned, was a donation from one who had foreseen our need. I must admit that in the weeks that followed, there were times that I wondered whether we had done the right thing.

One time that I was feeling down, I pictured myself as a naïve young man standing on the edge of a dense forest, chainsaw in one hand and axe in the other, with no funds or help coming yet still planning to clear the trees and the underbrush and build several cabins and a huge log building. This was basically the situation. Did this look insane? Was it insane? A sane man would not think this way! During the events that followed, I did sometimes wonder whether we were insane. But God saw the end from the beginning, as He always does, and He gave us the peace and the firm conviction that we were on the right track.

Strangely, the scene I have just described was a picture of what would soon occur: we would be alone. This book is a true record of events. I do not speak of these events with animosity of any kind, but to the Glory of God, since what we passed through proved to us that God is faithful to those who trust Him and believe in his power to supply what is needful in the work He has called them to do. This supply arrives in God's own way and in His own time. We can say without doubt or wavering that the Lord can be trusted to supply the needs of those who are called to serve Him. In fact, any of His children may have this assurance. This assurance was with both me and my wife when we made our decision to accept the challenge. Some of the what was to happen was simply unavoidable in people's lives. This is why we say the Lord gets all the credit. If, in the future, there comes a day that we depart from that principle, it will be the day that the camp will have to depend on human resources, which are like shifting sand and undependable.

Upon arriving in Chapleau, we learned that our Board of six members had diminished somewhat. As I mentioned, one of the six had, sadly, been asked to resign. One older gentleman had moved away, and another had moved as the result of job transfer. Only three remained. One of these was Gerry, and within months, in need of employment, he moved to the West to work for his brother. Then there was only one other Board member and me. Verna, the children and I stayed with Gerry and Sarah Martin for a few days until we were able to rent a cabin for the rest of the winter.

WALKING WITH FRIENDS

This depletion of Board members meant that the whole burden of setting up the Camp had shifted from the shoulders of six able-bodied men to those of two. Things looked grim. I wondered if the whole project should be cancelled. *Should I carry on (almost) by myself?* In reality, this was not my burden in the first place, although I had heartily agreed to do my part in bringing it to pass. Since there was nothing left for us back where we came from, the only thing we could do now was to find a place to live until I saw something positive in the future. My first responsibility was to provide the family with a house. After briefly searching Chapleau, I came to the conclusion it would be best to build one. We managed to buy a lot from the neighbour directly across from us, and I immediately proceeded to build using a set of plans I had brought with me. We had moved in the latter part of August, and once the dust had settled regarding the problem of the Camp, it was already the first of September. We needed a place to live; winter would soon be settling in.

I virtually worked alone unless I needed help for things I could not do. My neighbour was willing to help lift walls that I had built whenever it was convenient for him, which was not that often. We had made an agreement to keep track of the hours that he spent with me; then, when he needed help, I would return those hours working with him. In this way, no cash exchanged hands. However, an hourly rate was agreed upon so that, in the event that one or the other of us was unable to fulfill the hours he owed, he could pay cash for the other's help. With the spectre of winter on our doorstep, I worked as many hours as I could laying cement blocks for my foundation. How my arms ached the first two weeks! But then, how the Lord supplies!

Susan and Stephen searching for the house

One evening at about 7:00 p.m., as I was working on my house and on the third row of blocks, a stranger drove up. He was dressed in a pair of work overalls and he looked familiar. He didn't introduce himself but simply said, "How are you mixing the mortar?" I thought to myself, *Why do you want to know?* However, I politely replied, "Three of sand and one of mortar mix. But who are you?"

No sooner had I asked the question, distant memories began to crystallize of where I had met him before. It was at the men's conference in Guelph earlier that spring. I had been sitting by myself, waiting for the proceedings to start when a stranger slid in beside me. He said that he had heard we were planning to move to Chapleau soon. Completely taken by surprise, I had asked him who he was. He mentioned his name, but it slipped from my memory since I had no significant basis to remember it. I asked how he had heard we were moving to Chapleau, and he explained that he often visited there for his business selling insurance and had gotten to know the Christians there.

Back in the present, the man answered my question: "Alec Macdonald. I thought I would come to mix some mortar for you, since you are working alone." I was glad of his offer, and the conversation continued. From then on, with his extra pair of hands, the job moved along much faster. He stayed for a day or two, and then he left. Since that time, we've had a friendship which has lasted over the years. Often, after the house was built, Alec would arrive unexpectedly, open the front door and say, "Verna, have you got the tea kettle on?" His arrival was always like a ray of sunshine to us. He would stay a few days and then move on. He was in touch with the Lord and seemed to come when I needed encouragement most.

WALKING SHORT DISTANCES

When the hunting season was past, Verna and I and the kids moved into one of Jim Demers's cabins. Jim was a railroad man and had a few cabins that he rented to hunters and fishermen. Hunting season had just ended and he offered to rent us one at a reasonable price while I built my house. This was a great deal for us since the cabin was right next door to where I was building. The understanding was that we would have to move out once the spring fishing season opened. Jim must have kept his eye on how we were doing because he offered to bring building materials from Timmins for me whenever he had reason to go there. Timmins was roughly 120 miles away, but I could get better prices there on materials for the house. Toward the end of November, I had the foundation laid, the house framed, the roof on and windows covered with plastic. Then Verna and I went to the bush to cut wood to keep a fire going to prevent the footings from freezing. This also made it cozy for working during the winter months.

Firewood to make work cozy

Unfortunately, my exchange of working hours with my neighbour later became a burden to me. Because I needed extra help to lift some walls and do other things one man cannot do alone, our agreement was soon out of balance by several hours. Many times, I tried to repay some of those hours by doing some work for him but was rejected because he couldn't use the hours profitably. This became a personal burden to me and was a daily bother.

I decided I would level things out by paying him the cash value per hour as agreed upon. Since my funds were mostly used up in building, I prayed that the Lord would provide some employment for me so that I could settle the account and relieve the debt to my neighbour. The Lord answered by providing me with several hours of supply teaching at the local public school. My desire to pay the debt was in keeping with the will of the Lord in His Word: "Owe to no man anything, save to love one another" (Romans 13:8). I paid the debt and my mind was at peace. But, inevitably, that peace was shaken on occasion.

When you are involved in works of the Lord, there are times when tests of faith stare you in the face. In the north, we had sparse support for some months. I did not question why, but I knew we could not live long on $20 a month. Before we left Guelph, one of the elders said to me, "You may have to do some *tent-making* in the future in order to get by." I responded, "If we do, we know the Lord will take care of us."

WALKING WITH THE LORD

In the midst of our trying times, I spoke to the Lord, reminding Him that we could not live on this small amount for food, rent, gas, clothes and daily needs—as if He did not know that, already. He promptly responded, "You have money in the bank; spend it on your needs!" I knew He was referring to the $5000 we had brought with us and were counting on for building our house. By this time, however, most of it was used up anyway. We heeded His voice in our hearts, and when it was all gone, the Lord provided according to our needs. From then on, life became more exciting. We were walking on the water!

Throughout the winter, I worked on the house, wiring, plumbing, insulating and sheathing the inside with solid lumber. By the following May, our house was ready for occupancy. Alec Macdonald was sent by the Lord, and Lucy Weber, a personal friend of ours, was visiting at the time. They helped us move our stuff into the house. By this time, I had built all the permanent windows and also installed the glass. The house was quite comfortable, although it looked unfinished, with its bare plywood floors and interior walls covered only in new lumber. To this day, our daughter, Susan, recalls the green lumber walls. She reminds us that they were okay until the boards dried out and shrank. Then there was a half-inch space between each board.

Len Fex and his family moved away to Timmins at about this time. It was then necessary for me to take on the pastoral work in the small assembly as well, since there was no one else in it who felt capable of speaking.

WALKING IN UNCERTAINTY

The spring and summer were spent finishing the essentials of the house to make it more liveable. The concrete basement was poured and the septic system assembled and working. Up until now, by the good graces of my neighbour, I had been getting our water via a hose from his well across the road. However, a permanent well of my own was necessary now that we had moved into our house. In the Lord's proper timing, my neighbour met a well-driller at a restaurant and suggested I speak to him. We met the driller, who told me that his outfit used a carpenter's type of drill that could only reach about 15 meters in depth. I was somewhat dismayed but told him we were built on sand, and I wasn't sure of the depth. Then, getting interested, he said he could only drill a maximum of five inches in diameter, but that would allow us to get a four-inch submersible pump inside to lift the water. I agreed to let him try, and in a short while, his rig was set up on our front lawn. As he drilled, he worked in a pipe well casing which would stay there and constitute my well when he was finished.

The drilling went well and in about two hours he was as far down as he could go with his equipment. He pulled everything up out of the hole, and from the surface of the ground, we measured the level of the water. It was static at six meters and never fluctuated. The driller said, "Well, sir, you have a good well there, and it looks like the level will stay at six meters." This was good news; I would not need to go to the expense of buying a deep-well submersible pump. Happily, I thanked him and paid the bill which, as I recall, was minimal.

Since the water was static at 6 meters from the top of the ground, I could use a shallow-well pump and get closer to the water level by building a concrete box which would reach down about 2.4 meters from the top of the ground. Also, I could install a pump at that level in the basement of the house, making it only a lift of 3.6 meters from the water to the pump. From there, I could go directly into the basement of the house at the floor level. This was a perfect arrangement. As for the pump, there was no need to buy one since I had brought a shallow-well pump with me when we moved up in August. This was all in the foresight, wisdom and direction of the Lord. Praise His Name! Our next job was to go to Timmins and get sufficient supplies to put the whole system together. Soon enough, we were able to function properly on our own with our own water readily available. Having good, pure water on hand from our own well was a major problem off my hands.

Details concerning the Camp had been finalized, with a 21-year lease set up by the Ministry of Natural Resources. This was done prior to our arrival and before most of our board members had realized they would be moving away. Since the camp property was secure now, we planned on clearing a way into the site. In the summer of 1968, we took some of the local young people along, and Verna and I cut the trail into the proposed camp. At the same time, we decided where the road should go. We tried to keep in mind that if it went straight, there was a danger of speedsters coming in and seriously injuring a child; it was possible that a child might step out of the treeline and onto the road at the same time. To prevent this, we put several curves in the roadway. By directing it around well-established, stately evergreens, the beauty of the property was enhanced. We now had the Camp defined and could take a real interest in it.

That same summer, the only other Board member and I went to the Camp and laid out the areas for the cabins, etc. Strangely, his help evaporated after that, and then I really was left alone. It seemed his enthusiasm for the Camp had disappeared, and with no explanation. We had always previously had a good, warm relationship. This strangeness continued for some time. Later, I assumed that he had suddenly realized how much construction work would be involved in establishing the Camp, and how much time—perhaps it was more than he wished to give.

CHAPTER 4

Steadying the Waters

COMFORT FROM A FAITHFUL BROTHER IN CHRIST

As the months passed, we had gotten to know Alec quite well. As usual one day, he appeared at the front door and stuck his head inside. "Have you got the tea kettle on, Verna?" His voice was like a song from heaven! This manner of entrance and greeting was common among people of the Maritimes, Alec's home of years gone by. It seemed that the Lord had sent him to cheer me up and to suggest a solution to my problem. I mentioned that the Camp Board had dissipated, and I was alone. What should I do? Was this the will of God? Should we cancel the idea of a Christian camp, since we were by ourselves? Again, I was getting discouraged. I felt I was in a blind alley, that it had all been a big mistake!

But Alec was a positive thinker. He knew that the summer months were just ahead and that young teenaged boys would be planning their vacations. If they knew what was going on here, some would be excited about coming north to help clear the forest, learn about building cabins and do some fishing on the side. He suggested that I go ahead with the project. He reasoned that I could write a letter to several assemblies in southern Ontario. In the letter I could invite any strong teenaged boys to help do the work described and help us to reach our proposed goal of establishing the Camp. This suggestion was like a ray of light, giving me encouragement in my cloud of darkness. I moved forward on his advice, mentioning in the letter that it was a faith project.

Being involved in such a project, with no money to begin with or even to operate, kept us looking to the Lord. I knew the Lord must supply whatever was needed, both for ourselves personally and for the Camp's development. To arrive at this conviction, quite often one has to wrestle with oneself about whether one has sufficient faith to see things through. Unfortunately, my old doubts were returning, and depression was again settling in. Would the blind alley doubt be a reality? Was I only fooling myself? I often wondered, *Do I have sufficient faith to trust the Lord for all of our needs?* I often asked myself how we had arrived at this point, with no foreseeable income and daily expenses, like everyone else? Had I been foolish to leave a good teaching position back in Guelph to move to this and these circumstances in which we had to trust God for His supply in the days ahead? Should I back out, sell what I had and move back to teaching and the security of a monthly paycheque? Indeed, the very thought was comforting! However, when I was in such a state, these thoughts only led to confusion; they did not help the present situation. When I began to level out, then I would reason. *How can I be sure we would have security back there, out of the Lord's will? Life could be very different!* I was plagued with such thoughts until the Lord in His mercy brought to my mind some verses of Scripture He had given me some years back.

COMFORT FROM THE SCRIPTURES

First, I recalled again what God had said to Moses to encourage him to speak to Pharaoh. In Exodus 3:12, He gave him these words: "Certainly, I will be with you" [Or "With certainty, I will be with you"]. As it did Moses, this verse gave me great comfort, since God was giving me assurance of His presence.

The Lord gave us even more assurance to strengthen our faith. I recalled the verse He had provided when I had stood before the Dean of London Bible College, hoping to be accepted. The Dean had asked me if there was a verse of Scripture that had led me to want to enter the College and eventually the Lord's work. I had not expected such a request from him, but was supplied by the Holy Spirit with a verse I had always treasured, Joshua 1:9: "Have not I commanded you? Be strong and of good courage; do not be afraid, nor dismayed, for the Lord your God is with you wherever you go." This satisfied the Dean that my call had been authentic and also gave me confidence, because the Lord had given me what was needed by refreshing my memory.

These verses encouraged me afresh, as did Hebrews 13:5: "I will never leave you nor forsake you." And again, the Lord gave another verse that had strengthened me in the past, especially when I had to do something and lacked confidence in my ability to succeed. This was Habakkuk 3:19: "The Lord God is my strength; He will make my feet like deer's feet, and He will make me walk on my high hills." This verse above all others gave me the confidence I needed. With faith and confidence renewed, I pressed on with gusto, realizing the Lord would see us through and would not fail us in our needs, for after all, this was His work, and we were but His servants. Taking this position, I could confidently look to Him to supply all our needs for what lay ahead. I was ready to compose a letter and send it on.

CHAPTER 5

Stilling the Waters

Faithful Friends

A bright spot in our circumstances was when we met Jorma and Margie Saari and their little family. This was during the winter, while I was still building the house. I had needed some old white-pine boards to be planed for the inside-sheathing of my house. Jorma agreed to do this for me at Island Lake, where he lived and worked. Through our relationship, I had shared the good news of the Gospels with him and learned they were born-again Christians. We passed different aspects of the good news along to them and were invited to come to their home for Bible study. I should mention that, at this time, we were travelling weekly to Island Lake for children's meetings. After we had finished the work with the children, we would go to the Saari home to have a Bible study. For the rest of the evening, time seemed to fly by as we shared the riches we have in our Lord Jesus. Sometimes, at midnight, Jorma would say, "Margie, put on some more coffee!" We would continue sometimes until 2:00 a.m. These events encouraged us in the Lord throughout the winter. We became fast friends, and afterward, Jorma became one of our Board members. He also had a trucking business and hauled several loads of dressed lumber to various places in southern Ontario. In his generosity, he offered to backhaul, at no cost to us, various things that were needed for the Camp, like kitchen appliances and steel trusses for the second floor of the main lodge.

Before we got far into the building project, I enquired of Jorma where he thought I could get building materials at a reasonable price. We would need enough to build four cabins and to sheath the floors and roofs with solid lumber. He directed me to a retired man who had at one time owned a sawmill in Devon but had since gone out of business. He had quite a bit of well-seasoned lumber left over, and maybe he would sell it to me. I followed his directions and visited this man, explaining to him that we were in the process of building a children's camp. I asked if he had any lumber to sell. He took me to his weathered piles of two-inch and one-inch lumber. The wood was dry and straight and exactly what we wanted.

"How much will it cost me?" I asked. He said, "I'll sell it for $90 per 1000 board foot." This is the terminology for quantity used when selling lumber. Then I asked, "Do you want payment in advance, or later?" He replied, "Take what you need when you want it. Keep a tally of what you take and pay later." My heart lifted to the Lord with a big *thank you*. I could not have asked for better terms. With rejoicing, I filled the pickup with whatever I could carry, wrote it down and drove off. I realized that we were going against our principle of not buying on credit, but if no money was available to settle the bill, I was sure that some way or other, I would pay it with my own resources; I knew the payment would be assured.

We were greatly strengthened by the response we received from young fellows. Many practical and far-seeing mothers knew the appetites of their boys and asked what the approximate cost would be to feed their sons at the Camp. In return letters, I suggested that $12 weekly would be a big help. Consequently, according to the number of weeks the boys would stay, most mothers sent sufficient sums to feed them. Usually, there was an extra gift to help the project from the parent or their assembly. I also mentioned that there was good fishing in the lake where we were situated, and told them to bring along their fishing tackle. Some of them did, and whatever they caught usually went to subsidize our meals, since they had no means of getting the fish home unspoiled. We also found, to our surprise, that many caught fish measured 90cm to 100cm long—northern pike, of course.

In the letter, I mentioned that we would have a daily Bible study, so they should bring their Bibles. This proved to be a precious time each day and it fulfilled the vision we'd had for the camp. Charlie Shorten, whom I knew from the past, joined us for the whole summer. I took advantage of Charlie's walk with the Lord and asked him to supply the Bible studies each morning. As I think back on those times, I realize that I had laid quite a burden on him, but the Lord made him equal to the task and we had a good time each day. Bible study took up to an hour, and sometimes an hour and a half, each morning. This left me free to direct the task of building and to keep things moving. During the study, many questions were inevitably asked, and our time seemed to fly by.

Fighting with the bugs

HELP FROM AFAR

Before any help arrived, I had gone to the old gravel pit across the road and gotten our first load of gravel in readiness for putting in the concrete post foundations. Bob McLean from the assembly in Sarnia offered to come and help. He arrived early to join us in constructing the first cabin. Around the same time, Charlie Shorten, Alec Macdonald and his son, John, also arrived. Gerry Martin was still in the area and helped out as well. Together, we cut the trees and cleared the brush for the roads within the Camp. It was great to have our first meal over a campfire by the lake. I recall that, while clearing the brush and cutting down some trees, I had special visits with the Lord in which my heart was filled with His presence. This gave me full assurance that, in the years ahead, the camp would be a place of spiritual blessings in the lives of those who would attend. This would include adults as well as children.

First lunch at the Camp

Bob McLean came with his own sleeping quarters in the back of his covered pickup truck. He was quite a capable builder and stayed with us until the first cabin was built, and then, as I recall, did some work on the second. He was also quite an avid fisherman. One evening, out on the lake and enjoying himself, he hooked onto a *very* large pike. I think he said it was the "granddaddy" of them all. At the time, I was out on the lake myself in one of the canoes that Ken and Marg Dickson had sent up from Toronto. Bob wrestled with the fish, trying to get it into the boat, and then he yelled at me to quickly come and help him. I responded, paddling as fast as I could. But then I heard Bob say, "Ohhh, I should have waited!" He held up his fishing net, displaying the large hole that the fish had torn through it to escape. Every time thereafter that he described the event, he would say, "Well, that one has my name on it! I am coming back next year to claim it!"

In response to the letter we had sent out, we heard especially encouraging news from Sarnia, Ontario. Bill Abbot had a business in building sailboats and selling other kinds of boats, such as aluminum rowboats. He sent us a gift of a new aluminum rowboat with all the accessories for the workers to use and for their enjoyment when not working. Thanks be to the Lord and to Bill's generosity! Later, he sent two single-passenger sailboats as well.

Blow, ye winds, hi ho!

CHAPTER 6

The Dream Materializes

A PLACE FOR ACTIVITY

Upon hearing of the number of boys coming to assist us for the summer, we knew it was urgent that we get two cabins up as soon as we could. These would be 16 feet by 24 feet. One cabin would serve as a cookhouse with a stove, a gas refrigerator, food storage, an eating area, and be used for Bible study as well. It also would serve as sleeping area, curtained off at night, for Verna, Susan, Lyn and Mary Lucas, who were under our care at this time. We managed to get this one done first and the other one prepared to house the boys when they came.

It was a busy and tight arrangement for a while, but we did nicely. Upon the arrival of the boys, we set some to clearing the bush while others helped in the building of cabin 3, where the women and girls could sleep. It didn't take long for these things to happen, since with all of the boys there, it was quite a gang working. On the Lord's Day, we occasionally remembered the Lord in the same area where we had our regular Bible study, or else we travelled into Chapleau to meet with the believers there.

Heave ho!

Previously, we had known we would need proper outhouses. Jim Demers had offered to build these for us before the gang came. I brought them out on the little half-ton truck that had been donated. Jim had built these outhouses from the lumber he and I salvaged from old cabins; the Sheppard and Morse white-pine lumber company had agreed to give the lumber to us if we dismantled the cabins. Prior to the whole operation beginning at the campsite, Jim and I had gone to dismantle what was useable and bring the lumber home on our trucks.

Also, Jorma had built a cabin in the bush for his own use a few years before our enterprise at the camp and before we met him. The provincial authorities didn't like where he had built and had ordered the cabin taken down or destroyed. Jorma told us we could have all the lumber if we cared to remove it for him. One of the first jobs we did with the fellows who came to help was to go to the area, dismantle the cabin and bring what was useful back to Wildwood Bible Camp. Thanks again to Jorma!

At last, the pot was boiling, so to speak. Wildwood Bible Camp was becoming a reality, and we were moving ahead! Our son, Stephen, and I slept with the boys in the other cabin. Outside, we provided a personal washing-up area for those who did not want to use the lake. We all functioned within these conditions until the third cabin for the women was ready. Nobody complained. Lots of good food was prepared; the tasty fish meals Verna prepared especially kept the boys happy. Occasionally, she favoured us with some baked goods or a special desert. These surprised everybody, and we all enjoyed them. Every evening, there was a good campfire and singsong to finish off the day, or just a plain evening enjoying the lake.

A Place for Refreshment

As one might imagine, cutting down trees and piling up and burning branches and other brush works up a sweat. The remedy was a dip in the lake. This was always refreshing, but we needed something more to add new interest and challenge. Jorma, who was of Finnish origin, said that a good sauna bath after dirt, blackflies and sweating all day was very refreshing. He offered to build a stove that would be proper for a sauna bath if we wanted to put up a building in which a bath would be suitable.

I had had many a sauna in his bathhouse, and I agreed that it was a good idea. We had some lumber that had not quite made the cut for building the cabins. The boys were all excited to use it to construct the sauna. The bathhouse was mainly a project of the younger fellows in the evenings. Under Jorma's direction, the building was soon ready, and then Jorma installed the stove. The sauna was a huge success and was heated up every night, with everyone taking a turn. Usually about eight could go in at once. Occasionally, the temperature would reach well in excess of 130 degrees Fahrenheit. The longest one could be inside was about five minutes or less, rarely more. After you came out, the big event was to run down the boardwalk and dive into the cool lake. The sauna became a popular attraction over the years.

Likewise, one day we heard about an old abandoned building that was in a gravel pit about eight miles west of us down the road. It had been there for years. An outside party said we might as well take it, as it would only deteriorate in time. About six of us went to the pit, checked it over and decided we could easily dismantle it in wall sections. This done, we loaded it on a flat trailer and brought it to the Camp. We got the sections nailed back together before lunchtime. By suppertime, we were well on our way to having a simple foundation.

From then on, Verna and others used it as a handy laundry building for the old wringer washing machine somebody had given us for use at the Camp. Some years later, it was moved to a new location; today, it serves as a staff cabin. It has been refurbished on the inside with proper wall coverings and on the outside with suitable paint. Most people don't know its previous history.

A PLACE FOR SATISFACTION

Once the summer was over and everyone had left, we returned to our home in Chapleau, where I carried on with the bricklaying at the front of our house. It had been brought to a halt once the summer's activities were upon us. As I continued working at the brick, my mind went back to the number of cabins we had been able to see constructed. When everything was over and the bills were paid, we still had $85 in the Camp's account. I was rejoicing in what had been accomplished.

Suddenly, it dawned upon me that I had not yet settled for the lumber I had picked up at the beginning of the summer. I knew that the amount we owed him far exceeded what we had in the account. I quickly mentioned this to Verna and together we wondered what we were going to do. We prayed for the Lord to give us some direction. We wanted to be honourable in all that we did, especially in relation to the name of the Camp, so that it could maintain a good testimony as a Christian camp. Then, a peace seemed to settle over us concerning the matter. We both knew I had to go and settle up in some way. All the way out to Devon, I wondered how to handle the shortfall. But in His own peace-assuring way, the Lord spoke to my heart, saying, "This is my bill, not yours; I will look after it." Peace settled in again.

Upon arriving at Devon, I presented the tally to the man and said that I had come to settle our accounts. Under my breath, I added, "I don't know how." He looked at the tally and then said, "Instead of $90 a thousand board feet, I am only going to charge you $30 per thousand." That brought the bill to $175! And then, while I was still trying to recover from the relief and shock, he said, "I am going to give you a donation of $100, so according to my calculation, you owe me $75. My heart seemed to skip a beat. I thought, *Is it true, what he is saying?*

I sincerely thanked him, and at the same time a shiver went from the back of my neck and down my spine as I thrilled at the ways of the Lord. I wrote a check for $75 and went on my way, rejoicing in the sovereign ways of God. All was settled and we still were $10 to the good. What a great blessing it is to have the Lord assure you of peace and to serve Him! We thought we had reached a blind alley, unable to pay our bills, but the Lord proved it was not so—for He has no blind alleys!

CHAPTER 7

The Bringer of Good Things

Equipment for Ease of Working

As I recall those days and the work that was before us, not knowing in advance what our needs may be, how I praise Our Heavenly Father that He well knew His plan! He used many of his dear children to think of those items that would be needful in the days ahead and to suggest them to me. The Lord used Alec Macdonald in this vein of things. He was one of the Lord's choice servants, and he was always thinking ahead. He would arrive at the Camp with his little Vauxhall car loaded to the roof and on top with items he was sure we would need. He had to travel approximately 180 miles from where he lived on Highway 17 to the Camp. These were miles, not kilometres. It seemed that everything he brought found a place of usefulness.

Before the boys arrived for the second summer, one day Alec appeared at the door, asking his favourite question, "Verna, have you got the tea kettle on?" He wondered how we were doing at the camp. I said we are doing brush work whenever I got some help. He then said to me, "You know, if you had a small tractor at the camp to pull stumps and clean up a lot of the brush as the trees are cut, it would make the work a lot easier." I agreed! He said he knew where we could get a Massey Pony (a small tractor) for about $500. I was interested and the next thing we knew, we were headed south to Thessalon to see the tractor. On the way there, Alec mentioned that he had also found a large scoop that would be useful to skim off the roads around the camp, and that we could pull it with the tractor. "The cost of that has been taken care of." He didn't say by whom, but I could guess who had paid for it.

We arrived a few hours later and examined the little tractor. To my eye, it looked to be in good condition, so we made the deal. There were other implements that came with it, but once they were in the truck, there was no room for the tractor. I wanted to just leave the implements behind so we could load the tractor and move it to Chapleau that evening; we could pick up the implements on another day. But Alec had other ideas. He was sure he could drive the tractor to Chapleau that night while I took everything else in the truck. I objected, but he insisted, and how do you argue with a Scotsman? This would be a journey of 135 miles. So we got the tractor tank loaded up with gasoline and two extra jerry cans full of it. I had picked up other goods and chattels for the camp along the way, so I left at about 5:00 p.m., assuming Alec would be leaving at the same time.

FAITHFULNESS IN DELIVERING THE GOODS

Alec had it all planned to stop at a friend's place and eat supper with them (conjecturing that he would be asked to stay for supper) and then to get on the road to Chapleau. But his visit took about an hour, and he couldn't get away before 6:00 p.m. This was early May and the weather looked to be nice, so I was not concerned about whether he would be warm enough. However, I had misjudged the springtime temperature in that part of the country.

I arrived in Chapleau at our house around 9:30, unloaded the pickup truck and asked Verna for some supper. Then I said I was also going back to help Alec, as I didn't want him to be on the road all night. The tractor, travelling under its own power, was only capable of about 12 miles per hour, wide open. Assuming he had left at 6:00 p.m., Alec would be on the road for approximately 12 hours before he got here around 6:00 a.m., if everything went well. I knew Alec was diabetic and needed some energy every so often. Then I wondered, *How will he make it twelve hours without some source of energy?* I began to be concerned about him. I started out again at 10 p.m., having gotten gassed up again. As well, I took some coffee and sandwiches along for him.

Since I am not a fast driver and tend to be cautious, it was a good two hours before I sighted him. This was about 12:30 a.m. He was roughly halfway between Chapleau and Thessalon in an area that was quite hilly. As I came over a hill, I could see a very faint light moving back and forth, in effect cautioning any oncoming traffic about his presence on the road. This was a wise thing to do. Sure enough, it was Alec, waving his flashlight, the batteries nearly dead. I slowed down, pulled alongside of him and asked how he was. But there was no answer! It was obvious he was very cold. Fortunately he had a heavy raincoat on, but otherwise he was tired and cold.

Anyone living in the north of the province will be well quite aware that in early spring, the day can be quite pleasant, but then, in the dark of night, the temperature cools off quickly and can be downright cold. This was springtime, so I knew that here was a man who would be glad to get into a warm truck. He would certainly enjoy the sandwiches and hot coffee Verna had sent along for him.

Alec was about sixty-five years old at this time, and I was about forty-two. He got off the tractor and I loaded him into the truck. The engine was belting out comforting heat into the cab. Then I searched and found a low impression beside the road into which I could back the truck. Next I positioned two wooden planks I had brought for this purpose and proceeded to load the tractor onto the truck. Soon it was chained down and we began our long drive home.

I drove very cautiously so as not to overbalance the load and throw the whole thing into the ditch. Consequently, we arrived home shortly after 4:00 a.m. and wearily crawled into bed. How I thanked the Lord for this dear brother, who so often came alongside to help me in our need and discouragement! Typical of Alec, he was so anxious to put the tractor and new implements to work out at the Camp that he was up at about 7:00 a.m. the next morning, itching to clean up some brush and maybe to try it pulling some stumps.

Alec and Stephen on the Pony

There was something about Alec and his ways that always struck me as very funny. I don't think he knew it, but I found him to be very humorous; he was the lighter side of our relationship. In regards to the early days of our work at Chapleau, he would always show up at a time that I needed help or encouragement. In this, I was convinced the Lord had sent him. He was self-employed, so he was free to come and go as he pleased. That was several years ago, and now he is with the Lord, having passed into His presence in 1993. No doubt Alec was greeted by the many souls he pointed to Christ over his lifetime, as well as by the worthy approval of His Lord: "Well done thou good and faithful servant, enter into the joy of your Lord."

Trying out the Pony

That is the story of one tractor. The story of another is just as thanksworthy and was also the provision of the Lord. The little

Pony tractor was very useful for small stuff, but it could not help us much with heavier work. Something larger would make everything go much more easily.

A Neighbour Driven by Curiosity

Milton

Close to the entrance to the Camp, perhaps just 800 feet away, we had a neighbour whom we assumed was a trapper of small, fur-bearing animals. When the construction started, he would wander over to ask what we were doing. His name was Milton. Occasionally, we would take the time to stop in and say hello. His shack was located near the highway, hardly visible from the road. It was adjacent to a small lake called Edna where he got his supply of drinking water. His quarters were half in and half out of the ground. The walls consisted of logs crudely fitted together horizontally, and the roof was made of large scraps of rusted sheet metal laid loosely together, not close enough to keep the rain out. As one approached the entrance, one saw a descending stairway of split logs crudely fitted together. There were about six steps down to a short, weathered door, barely five feet tall and fitted with a padlock. This was locked whenever Milton was away. The walls were also constructed of logs crudely fitted together, some overgrown with green moss. It was obvious they were beginning to rot.

Whenever I or others visited him and the padlock open, we usually hollered, "Hello, Milton, are you there?" If he was, he would partially open the door and squint from behind it. If he knew you, he would open the door wide. Visitors were always welcome. Once he had gestured you inside, you would become immediately aware of a pungent smell coming from a large pile of opened food cans thrown roughly into the corner. Of course, the contents had all been devoured. To the right of this garbage pile sat an old, small iron stove located by the only window. This constituted the southern wall, which let in the sunlight and also, to some degree, the heat of the sun. As your eyes followed the stovepipe, you would see that it passed through a loosely cut hole in the roof, around which you could see some blue sky. The dimensions of the single room were about 10 feet square, and when you were inside, you'd feel crowded in. Against the far wall, opposite the stove, was Milton's narrow bed. The covers were usually thrown back, revealing sheets that had not been laundered lately. The bed was placed in such a way that the raindrops coming through the nail holes in some parts of the steel roof would miss it. Obviously, since the roof was flat, the ceiling was, too; the steel sheets served as both ceiling and roof. The height inside the dwelling was about six feet in most places because of the unevenness of the earthen floor. Looking at the structure of the building from the inside prompted the question, *How does he keep warm in here, especially during winter?*

If you asked him to, he would get out his old violin and play it for you. He had a strange way of holding it. He held it upright with his left hand so he could depress the strings while resting the base of it upon his knee. In this position, he moved the bow back and forth horizontally, like a saw. It was always obvious when he played that he was enjoying himself.

Our visits to his abode were occasional because we usually saw Milton as he was walking toward the Camp on his way to see what was of interest to him there, especially to see the cause of all the noise that day. He had a strange gait; he would walk leaning forward, sort of on the balls of his feet, in a semi-trot. Picture it if you can! Some said that he walked that way because he had frozen his toes at one time. Whenever he knew there was an activity going on over in the camp, he would make his way over. Then we would get the latest news of the goings-on in his world.

Before the large dining hall was built, Verna usually remembered Milton's birthday by baking a special birthday cake. He would come over and we would sing "Happy Birthday" to him. Invariably, this would bring tears to his eyes. What was common to us was rare for him. He was touched by this kindness, especially when we all sang to him. You may wonder why he lived in such conditions. Some said that he had had difficulties in his marriage, whatever that might mean. Some years after, he became eligible for Old Age Security pension status, and his life became much easier, since he eventually moved into Chapleau.

CHAPTER 8

Greater Muscles of Steel

Covetousness or Opportunity

South of Chapleau, there was an Indian reserve located 25 miles away. We had been out there on several occasions, taking used clothing to the Indians (who are now known as First Nations peoples), and to hold a form of Daily Vacation Bible School (DVBS) with the children. result, we became fairly well-known. On one such trip, I noticed a fairly new International B-414 farm tractor with a flat rear tire parked off the roadside. I had seen it there before on several occasions when we went out to the reserve.

Ideas often came into one's head, especially about how useful items such as this could be at the Camp; I am convinced that they were not necessarily our own, but of the Lord. I decided to turn aside and examine the tractor more closely. Children had been playing on it and the gas tank was overflowing with sticks, stones and sand. The electrical wires had been torn free from the spark plugs and were just hanging there. As I had noticed before, the main rear tire was flat. Other than that, though, it looked as though it could be restored. I was puzzled as to why it had quit in the first place and been left in the ditch for the last few years, so I decided to contact the chief, Fred Neshawabin, and ask if they would consider selling it to me. His response was, "No, it is not for sale." "Thanks anyway, Fred," I said. "But if you change your mind, let me know. I would be interested in buying it as it is." This seemed like a blind alley. We would carry on doing the best we could at the Camp.

Opportunity or Junk

Just before the heavy snowfall that year, I got a call from Fred at the reservation about the tractor. I guessed that he'd had been doing some thinking about my offer. "Mr. Millson, I am calling about that old tractor in the ditch out here. Do you still want it?"

I told him I was still interested and asked, "How much do you want for it?"

"This tractor isn't up to much, so you can have it for $200."

"Fine, I'll take it," I replied. "I will give you $100 now and the other hundred when I pick it up. Is that okay, Fred?"

"Yes, that's fine. Would you send a taxi out to pick us up? Then we can stop at your house to pick up the money."

I phoned for the taxi and sent them to pick Fred up. About two hours later, he was at the door. Best of all, he was bearing some good news. "Mr. Millson, that tractor is in bad shape. Just give us $100 for it and that's fine."

I replied, "That's great, Fred. I will give you $50 now and the other $50 when I pick it up."

Again, the Lord had opened the blind alley of their denial to sell it, and at a good price.

I proceeded to order a new inner tube. During the two weeks

we waited for it to arrive, there was a good blow of snow, and now there were about six inches lying on the ground. Once the inner tube arrived, I built a proper tongue so that I could fasten the pickup solidly to the tractor in order to pull it home behind the truck. Then, with the tongue and proper tools, I went out in the midmorning of a sunny day to install the new tube in the tractor's wheel. I gave Fred the other $50 before touching it. Nothing was making me suspicious, but I wanted to seal the deal in case there was a change of mind. This was only good business.

JUNK OR ANTICIPATION

My first job was to jack up the rear end of the tractor just slightly above the ground. This would enable me to turn the wheel so I could remove all of the bolts holding it in place. Once it was off the tractor, I next had to wrestle with it in order to position it properly on the ground. To envision the problem I had, you must know that my height is five feet seven inches. The wheel reached to about my upper chest and was quite heavy. However, I managed, and it helped me work up a sweat to overcome the cold that was settling in. The next problem involved separating the old tire from the rim to remove the old tube. This was done with a heavy sledgehammer and some old tire irons.

The next part of the job was like a nightmare. This was struggling to get the old tube out and the new one inside the tire. Filling the tube with air using a small hand pump and getting it back on the tractor would be comparatively easy, although time-consuming. But getting the tube out of the tire was some job when working by myself. Eventually, the hard part was done and I wrestled the wheel back on the tractor. I was then ready to see how the little truck could handle the job of pulling the heavy, lifeless tractor behind it, dragging it home.

I secured the tongue I had made to the truck and tractor, and then I began my long, slow journey home. It was about 3:30 p.m., and the sun was getting lower in the sky. However, I realized that because we were so far north, dusk was much longer than I was used to in southern Ontario. The sun seemed to take longer to set here than it did farther south. This was to my advantage because I had no travelling lights for moving when it was dark; it would have been illegal to travel on the highway without them. As it was, I had secured a slow-moving vehicle sign on the back of the tractor, as farmers do when moving their implements down the road in the daytime.

As I began my journey home, everything was going according to plan, but I could go no faster than second gear in the little truck. The high whine of the engine was monotonous, but at least the truck was moving. I had no engine power to tow it in high gear, so I settled down to a slow ride home in second gear. First, I had to go seven miles over a gravel road covered in six inches of snow. Then, having reached the highway, I would be able to move faster. My clothes were wet and I was cooling down just sitting in the truck. However, I was still moving, and my prize, securely fastened to the truck, was following obediently behind. I smiled with a satisfied grin. Things were easier on the highway. From here on out, I had about 18 miles to go to reach home and the comfort of a warm fire. I knew my dear wife would be waiting for me with a good, tasty dinner. She usually had the uncanny ability to prepare exactly the meal I was hoping for when she knew what I had been working at. I needed dinner right now, considering the hard slogging I had experienced fighting with the tire. But it was worth it to get this tractor in shape again. How much easier it would be for heavy jobs at the Camp!

But now, there was another fear nagging at me. Coming up on the highway was the big hill about ten miles ahead. The daylight was diminishing since it was the end of November, and it was getting colder. The snow on the highway was well-packed, making it somewhat slippery. Anyone reading this account may not realize that winter conditions in northern Ontario are much different from those in the southern area of the province. The day can change from bright and pleasant to freezing in a matter of hours. Where I had been working on the tractor, the snow had become wet and slushy from the sun and from my efforts wrestling the tire off and back on again. In the process, my clothes had become wet and soggy at the knees and seat. People often tell me that my hands are cold when we greet one another. On that day, they were especially so. I was looking forward to the moment when I would pull into our driveway with the tractor in tow behind. How long would it be before I could have that satisfaction?

Anticipation or Failure

The big hill I feared loomed just ahead, almost like a dreadful spectre. I got about halfway up it when I felt the truck losing its momentum. Then it came to a dead stop, the tires spinning. I was on clear ice created by recent heavy traffic. What was I to do? My spirits were beginning to sink! The tractor was pulling hard on the level. Now it was on a hill, I was helpless. I could not move over to the side of the road to clear it for any traffic that might want to pass. I could not back up as everything would jackknife and block the road even worse. I began chastising myself for not having had the foresight to put a few shovelfuls of sand in the truck before I had left home. Oh, why hadn't I done that? I felt I was at the end of the trail. Then something happened that will never be erased from my memory.

I waited for about a minute. Then I laid my head on the steering wheel, shivered once or twice and prayed, "Lord, you know the reason I am here is not for me, but for You, and this is Your work. I am cold and hungry, and I need to get the tractor over this hill and home. In Jesus' name I pray, please help me." Then I put the truck in gear and unbelief, expecting the wheels to spin on the ice. But to my joy and relief, the truck began to move. It went over the hill with the tractor coming behind. Have you ever seen a happy boy before? You would have seen one sitting behind the steering wheel of that truck that day. From then on, I was a firm believer that God still performs miracles. I had been hazy about it before, but now I was convinced. It is to this glory of God that I write this account. I was serving the Lord and I learned well the lesson that God has no blind alleys.

It was only about three-quarters of an hour later that I turned into our roadway up the small hill to our house. My destination was in sight. A prayer of thanksgiving was in order, and I joyfully gave it to the Lord for the way He had miraculously brought me over the hill and home. I uncoupled the tractor, manoeuvred the truck behind it and gently pushed it into our garage. I could work on it in warm conditions.

When dinner was over and I was sitting in the easy chair in the living room, my thoughts ran to what had happened about an hour before. I relived the event of the truck starting from a dead stop, then regaining traction and slowly but steadily going over the hill. I reasoned that someone must have been pushing. Could it have been one of God's special angels, commissioned to assist me in going over the hill? Why not? We believe other miraculous events in the Bible, which is God's inerrant word. Why not believe he sends miracles for our desperate needs today? Again, I was further convinced that when you are working with God and doing your best, there are no blind alleys. I mused further over my conviction that God had special plans for the tractor at Wildwood Bible Camp. It had been regarded by others as being in bad shape and valueless. But this proved untrue once it was restored and set to the tasks of which it was capable. I could not help but realize that this was also a symbol of what God can do with anyone He restores to His proper design. Isn't that what the gospel of Jesus Christ does in a fallen man's life? I believe it is. He did it in mine.

The Scripture declares plainly that God created man to be perfect and useful in His plan, but our first parents corrupted themselves by disobedience. Consequently, upon their being separated from God, death followed, and with it, corruption. Man and his descendants fell under the judgment of God because of sinfulness. The judgment was, "The soul who sins shall die" (Ezekiel 18:4). It also says that "All have sinned." This rendered mankind useless to God, destined for His scrap heap, which is hell. Like the tractor, he was "not up to much," as Fred had confessed, and was not useful to God as he was. However, God loved man! In order to restore him to usefulness, His Son took the judgment for our sins. Therefore, sin was judged, and we could go free. Through faith in Him who died for our sins, we can now be born again and made new creations in Christ Jesus. Thus we can now be made useful to God again. There is much more to this wonderful story.

It took half a day to get to the inside of the tractor's engine to see why it had been abandoned and parked on the side of the road for children to play on. When I did, I realized why it had stopped, although the reason had been unknown to its former owners. A valve ring, which fits very tightly into the engine block, had come out so the engine could not start properly, let alone run. It was simple and inexpensive to repair. I simply cleaned everything out and lined the ring up to go back into the hole where it belonged. Carefully, with some pressure, I pushed it back into its proper place. The other problems were relatively minor. It was not long before we had a fine, running tractor. Before taking it to the Camp, we gave it a fresh coat of paint. Its original cost had probably been about $8,000 when it was new—maybe more. But for us, it had cost only $100, plus a little bit of paint. Thank you again, Lord Jesus!

Our $100 tractor

Loss or Profit

The winter months went by, and in early spring, as I was driving into Chapleau, I noticed an old green five-ton dump truck with partially broken side racks. The truck had been sitting there for a few years and was certainly not eye-catching. The previous owner had died of a heart attack. I had noticed it many times before; it was just one of this man's possessions. But on this occasion, I was particularly drawn to it. Since it looked fairly useful yet, I wondered if his widow would sell it. I had visions of how useful it would be for hauling gravel from the pit and for other major things such as hauling crooked logs into the sawmill and exchanging them for lumber.

When I enquired, she said she had been thinking a lot lately about selling it and proceeded to relate to me in the form of a run-on sentence, "John, my husband had overhauled the engine and got it in good running order, checked everything else on it, even the brakes and lights, and then he got this severe pain in his chest, and it was not long after that he died, so I just left it there." It seemed to me that her thoughts had all been previously arranged so that, if someone enquired about the truck, she could clearly speak on all its good points. I could not fault her for that. She seemed like an honest woman. She continued, "It is no use to me, and now that John is gone I would like to sell it." I then enquired in French, *"Combien d'argent?"* ("How much money?") She said, "I'll sell it for $250."

"If I bought it, could I drive it away today? I mean, right now?" I asked.

"If you had a new license you could. It runs all right, at least it did before John died."

After taking the details, I left, picked up Verna and went and got a license. In the next hour, I paid for the truck, got behind the steering wheel and drove it home. Verna, in turn, drove the car home. I took a good look at the tires on the truck and noticed that one of the front ones was larger than the other. It did not affect the steering, yet it looked strange when it was coming toward you. But what difference was it to me if one tire was larger than the other? The wheels still went 'round, and it would do nicely for what I had in mind at the Camp. As soon as Jorma saw it, though, he sported a broad grin and said, "Ron, where did you get the truck?" I proceeded to tell him why I had bought it and for how much. He shook his head as he looked at it. He was used to buying new trucks for his business, ones that had new, matching tires.

I got the thing home and into my yard where I could crawl under it and take a good look. Everything seemed sound, so I proceeded to make plans about when to take it out to the Camp. Previously, Jim Demers had offered us a small building for which he had no use anymore. He had asked whether we could use it at the Camp, and I replied that I was sure we could.

Our $250 five-ton truck

But how would I get a heavy building onto the truck all by myself? I puzzled over it for a while and then realized that I could use the hydraulic lift on the truck to load it. First, I managed to tilt the building backward, as if I were going to push it over on its end. I propped it there securely, then lifted the flatbed of the truck with the hydraulics as if I was dumping a load. Then I backed the truck towards the tilted building, secured a chain around it and hooked the chain tightly to the truck. I lowered the hydraulic lift and the weight of the truck bed going down lifted the building onto the flatbed. I got behind the building and, by wiggling and pushing it, moved it farther onto the truck bed, where I could secure it with ropes and haul it out to the Camp. When I got there, I used the hydraulic system in the same way to unload the building safely without damaging it.

CHAPTER 9

Looking at Another Year

NEWER INTERESTS AND EVENTS

Happily, at about this time, Terry and Jackie Myland had moved into town and started attending the chapel. We became close friends, and they said that they were saved at about this time. Terry was very dependable, and I found Jorma to be the same, so with their consent, I added them both to the Camp Board. Another member was Herman Martin, a retired farmer from Wallenstein. Later, my brother-in-law, George Howard, who married Verna's sister Dorothy, also joined the Board. George was from Sarnia and skilled at building and many other things. Both he and Dorothy had taken a keen interest in the camp from the beginning. (Eventually, Dorothy would direct the girls camps for a year.) Later still, Don Pipe from Toronto expressed interest in the work, so he also was added as a Board member. This gave the Camp combined wisdom for steering in the right direction. We had very little money on hand, but it was sufficient to pay for the building materials needed from day to day. We had determined not to borrow money or charge credit for anything we could not pay for in the foreseeable future. This was a policy that all members of the Board appreciated.

One day in spring, Terry arrived at the Camp with quite a large number of red pine trees. They were small, the size used for planting as second growth. None of these evergreens grew naturally at the camp. Terry planted them to encourage growth in areas where trees had already been removed, so that new growth could be established. When red pines mature, they are tall stately trees, beautiful to behold. Terry had access to such trees since he was in the employment of the Ministry of Natural Resources. Their business was to encourage reforestation where trees had been removed. Terry had become quite familiar with Wildwood Bible Camp and was now hooked on it! His father, mother and younger brother came to visit and got involved in the various jobs that needed to be done.

In the writing of this account, I have failed to mention by name many different men and women who faithfully contributed their skills and talents in labouring for the Lord. This is because my memory fails me; I am unable to recall with the necessary accuracy all the details of what they accomplished. However, God remembers, and He is no man's debtor.

I want to say what a joy and blessing it was to have them there and to work with them. Many of the women served with Verna in the kitchen, while the men worked with me. Whether counselling during the Camp sessions or working in other areas, they were faithful in ensuring that everything that needed to be done was done. They pitched in and worked with a pure desire to be a part of what the Lord was doing at Wildwood.

Our Own Electrical Power

We precut as much building material as we could at our house in Chapleau before hauling it out to the site, but much still needed to be cut by hand out there. We had no connection to Ontario Hydro's power lines since none were close by. We often dreamed of having a power unit to facilitate our building on site, so we searched for one within our means. We managed to find a small gas-driven alternator, although I can't recall exactly where we found it. It was a four-cylinder inline gas engine which directly connected to a 9000-kilowatt generator, making it a solid unit. It was manufactured in this way when it was new. I decided to build a small weatherproof shelter in which to house it and also to locate it centrally to our general needs.

For a foundation, I sunk four cedar posts to secure the building. Everything seemed just fine as we bolted the unit solidly to the wooden floor. Within a few weeks, however, I saw my mistake. When the engine was operating, it set up a vibration that created a "bounce" in the alternator. This also created a spark which, in time, affected the armature, putting it out-of-round and thus causing it to stop producing electricity. What was I to do? Were we back to using handsaws to construct our cabins?

One day, the Lord gave me the direction to take the armature to Simon Oulette in Chapleau. He had a small garage for repairing his own heavy equipment and he had done some work for us opening the roads to get into the Camp during winter. I took the armature to him and explained our situation. It was not long before he had it back in top shape and able to produce power again. As usual, he charged me nothing, since he supported the purpose of the camp. God bless him! When the Camp was ready for children, Simon's own young daughter attended. Eventually, we built a structure that housed a solid concrete base on which we could mount the alternator and prevent any vibration. This became known as "the generator building." It met our needs, but due to voltage loss, it was limited when it came to construction at a distance.

MOVEABLE ELECTRICAL POWER

On a trip to southern Ontario, we called on Ken and Marg Dickson. Their daughter, Susan, had been with us doing Daily Vacation Bible School work with the children in small communities outside of Chapleau in the summer of 1968. The intent of this work was to gather local children together during the summer months to play games with them and to teach them Bible stories. They had often encouraged us to visit them, so we finally did so. Marg asked us if we had any needs for the Camp. I replied that we had often wished we had a small moveable generator to provide us with electricity on site. I explained that this would be useful both for building (we could move it from one place to another) and for later use around the Camp, wherever power was needed. "How much do they cost?" Marg asked. I said that I could get a new one that was a combined generator and welder for about $500. She promptly wrote out a check for that exact amount. In later days, Ken and Marg provided several canoes—a total of eight, as I recall.

I thanked the Lord inwardly for His faithfulness, and then I thanked Marg and Ken for their generosity, both at that moment and in the past. I left Toronto that day with the new unit on board. However, I faced a minor problem, namely, How were we going to move the generator around from place to place? We would need it for power in one place and then to do welding in another place, and the thing weighed about 200 pounds. It was too awkward and heavy to carry. On the drive home, the solution came to me. We needed to mount it on a little short-tongued trailer with rubber tires—but where to find one of those? This question was answered on a trip to the Planer area of Chapleau. I happened to see a small used axle with rubber tires already mounted, behind a resident's house in that area. On enquiry, I learned I could buy it for $25. I paid the price, loaded it in the truck and soon had the new alternator mounted onto it and ready for use.

A Washing Machine for the Taking

The next thing we needed was an electric washing machine. Since the Lord never lets us down, we kept our ears open for whatever might come up. It was not long before one was donated to us. Someone had just bought a new washing machine and was asking around whether anyone needed a used one. They wanted to be rid of it rather than leaving it lying around, so it was there for the taking. I believe it was Elsie Pellow who suggested that maybe it would be useful at Wildwood Bible Camp. She mentioned it to us, and it wasn't long before we had our electric washing machine. Once again, thank you, Lord. You always take care of our needs.

A Floating Boardwalk

A summer camp for children and adults is a suitable attraction for waterfront activities. In the early days, before any children came, we located several used 45-gallon drums that were ours just for picking them up. These had all been made rustproof with the application of paint on the exterior. We used them to make a suitable dock by floating them in the water underneath some wood. The dock was great for sunning oneself on after a swim. In later times, the dock was expanded.

At the end of that first summer constructing the cabins, etc., our work was done for the year. The end of the second summer brought a similar satisfaction. We could look with joy upon what the Lord had accomplished in His supply in the forms of both financial aid and physical help. Once everybody had left for home, the grounds seemed full of a lonely quietness that was almost unbearable. This great summer had come to an end, and our dream was becoming a reality.

CHAPTER 10

An Uninvited Guest

Verna's Big Surprise

One morning, during Junior Girl's Camp that summer, Verna had risen at 6:00 a.m. as usual and made her way through the morning mist to the kitchen to get breakfast started for the campers. When she stepped inside the kitchen, she found a terrible mess. An intruder had had a field day scattering things all over. She saw that the white-sugar container had been upset and its contents were spilled all over the floor. Other articles were scattered around, but the plastic brown-sugar barrel was missing. Then she noticed the screen was missing from the window by the door at the porch-end of the kitchen. This must have been how the invader had gotten in. She assumed it was a bear and quickly returned to our cabin to wake me and tell me what had happened. Others were getting up by this time and they joined in the excitement. Soon enough, the news had spread through the entire camp of girls. Another problem loomed into view: How would Verna prepare breakfast for everyone? Including the staff, there were 40 mouths to feed. Was this another blind alley? But

Verna called on her ingenuity and did manage to feed everyone that morning.

I went in search of the brown-sugar barrel and found it behind our most distant cabin. It was now full of tooth holes made by the bear's cleaning it out. Verna said there had been about six inches of brown sugar in there. Interestingly, I found a large tapeworm on the ground near the empty barrel. It appears that even bears need a good cleaning-out once in a while. That morning, I went into Chapleau to tell the Ministry of Lands and Forests about our visitor. They were the provincial authority that dealt with nuisance wildlife. They informed me that they would be out later that day to "move it out." In mid-evening, true to their word, two men from the Ministry arrived, planning to wait around until the animal returned after dark. We all waited in the kitchen, which adjoined the food storage area where Mister Bear had helped himself.

The bear had gotten into the kitchen through the window beside the back door of the kitchen storage area. The window looked out over a small porch that was about six feet square and two feet off the ground. Three steps led up from the ground to the porch. Tantalized by some delicious odour, the bear had knocked the screen out and crawled in through the window frame.

Patiently and quietly, we waited until about 10:00 p.m.. When darkness was upon us, I noticed a lot of noise coming from the nearby girls' cabin; they were excited about the expected bear. This cabin was next to the kitchen, so I strolled over and whispered into the window, "Be quiet or the bear may not come!" Then I quietly walked back toward the kitchen and, as usual, proceeded to climb up the steps. But as soon as my foot hit the first step, there was a loud noise to my right, where the garbage cans were sitting. It was dark, so I hadn't seen that the bear was close by. It must have been startled by the sound of my footstep, because it then attempted escape. I must have been right beside it at that moment. The loud noise was the sound of the bear trying to get away but slamming into our daughter's old toy baby buggy. The buggy flew about 10 feet away, and then the bear was gone.

On hearing the noise, those in the kitchen made their way out to the back porch, where the bear had been moments before. The officers from the Ministry said the bear would come back, so we all stood on the small back porch whispering and chatting for about five minutes. The night was pleasant and a full moon shone brightly when it wasn't shadowed by clouds. Occasionally, the moonlight reflected off the surface of the still lake, clearly illuminating the beach.

Lloyd Morris, nicknamed "Shorty" because he was so tall, originated from Chapleau and had been with us for most of the summer. He quietly joined us on the back porch. Shorty had done quite a bit of moose hunting in the past, and he had his rifle in hand. He had been thinking that the rifle might be handy if the bear came into sight. The atmosphere was tense as we quietly waited. Suddenly, Shorty spotted the bear silhouetted by the moonlight as it slowly walked along the shoreline of the lake. The moon lit the bear's form almost as clearly as daylight. Shorty, who knew the visitors from the Ministry quite well, took charge of the situation. He raised his rifle and, with the bear in his sights, pulled the trigger. With a loud squall, the bear ran for about 20 feet, then dropped to the ground. "Good job, Shorty!" hailed one of the men from the Ministry. "That took care of him!" With that, our guests left for Chapleau, saying they'd be back the next day to take the bear away. The night's excitement gradually died away, and everyone went to bed.

The Talk of the Town

In the morning, many wanted to see what a dead bear looked like, our son, Steve, included. He pointed with his finger at where the bullet had entered the body. The area was alive with campers all asking for details of the night before. By this time, rigor mortis had set in and the bear was quite rigid. Somebody suggested that we get the rocking chair and set the bear in it. Almost immediately, everyone ran for their cameras and started to shoot the bear again, but not with bullets this time. Many photos were taken of the unfortunate bear sitting peacefully in the rocking chair, with no place to go, its tongue hanging out as though it was gasping for its last breath. It gave it the appearance that it was even enjoying its stay at the camp. After all, its stomach was full of tasty brown sugar from the night before.

Our uninvited guest

That morning, excitement was high, since the campers would have an exciting story to tell when they got home about the night a bear visited the Camp's kitchen and helped himself to what it could find. In memory of this exciting night, the bear in the rocking chair became the symbol of Wildwood Bible Camp for a few years. A picture of this was skilfully drawn and used on the front of our camp brochures.

The bear episode may seem rather grisly to some people, but in our circumstances we had 50 to 60 children under our care, and with a bear of an unknown temperament in our immediate vicinity, we were taking no chances of any child being seriously injured or even killed. The Ministry of Lands and Forests generally move them out, and could have done so, but for some reason allowed the animal to be destroyed. When I had called them in I mentioned we had several children under our care and did not want to see any of them endangered by a hungry bear. As well, this could have quite easily shut our ministry down if any child might have been mauled by a hungry bear wandering into our area searching for food. Their option at the time was to allow it to be destroyed, rather than moved elsewhere. This event took place 44 years ago and sometimes the bear population needed to be reduced to maintain the balance in ecology.

CHAPTER 11

Outgrowing Our Space

BULGING AT THE SEAMS

As the Camp developed, interest in our community increased. Occasional visitors would stop in from Chapleau and elsewhere. Soon, adults saw that the Camp was a desirable place to send their children, and enrolment increased. As one might expect, it soon transpired that our kitchen and dining area, which measured 16 feet by 24 feet, was too small to feed all the campers at once. Meal times were extremely crowded, to say the least. We soon started thinking about erecting larger buildings.

I received a letter in springtime from Vic Northey of London, Ontario. Vic was from Egerton Street Gospel Chapel, and he said that a few of them would make themselves available to come and work if they were needed. I knew Vic was an elder in the church; in view of the present need, he would round up the right fellows to come and do the job.

Much thought went into what we should do. The idea of a log building kept invading my mind and visions. I presented this idea to others and all seemed to be in favor of it. But where would we find and obtain sufficient logs for what we needed? We had no supply of our own. Here again, we had worries of a blind alley.

Crowded girls camp

Full boys camp

We reasoned that the most sensible place to enquire would be the Ministry of Lands and Forests, or some similar governmental office. At Lands and Forests, I received the direction that I needed. I spoke to the officials about our plans and our need of logs, and asked about the number of good, straight evergreens beside our property. Could we use them? They told me about a lumber company in Chapleau that had the cutting rites in that area, and suggested if we asked them, they might let us have the trees. Then we could pay the Ministry for the stumpage we used. Within the hour, I went over to the office in question and posed the same question. When the authority heard where we were located and what we were doing, he gladly answered, "Sure, take all you need and don't worry about it; we will pay the stumpage fee." I thanked him sincerely and carried on with my other business. As I left their office, I realized gratefully that the Lord had answered our need once again. Now that the logs were all settled, I proceeded to line up some help so we could begin clearing land and cutting logs. I contacted Vic, described the job we had in mind and said I could use their help.

Crowded out with Logs

First, I had to decide on the size of the building. I could envision it in my head, but I found it difficult to put on paper. I decided to build something pleasing to the eye and practical for our needs. The urgent question now was where to put the building. We needed to decide this immediately, before the incoming helpers arrived. We managed to settle this matter by the time the fellows arrived, and we went right to work on this new major project of clearing the land.

Several of them had come north in one car, among them Vic, Stan Adams, Charlie Robinson, Charlie Shorten and his son Dave. These were men we had known for years. They were willing to brave the blackflies and to keep at the job. Someone suggested that we all get up at 4:00 a.m. and work until the bugs got bad. We could then take the rest of the day off. This would make the work much more enjoyable, and we would accomplish more in the long run. Everyone agreed, so we switched to this new schedule. Once we'd cleared the area for the new building, we were ready to start bringing in some logs. We did this while all the men were still with us, since the previous job had been completed so swiftly. I went to the area adjacent to the Camp to find some tall, straight logs suitable to our need. The men watched me select the trees and blaze them with an axe so they could see what type of trees were suitable for our needs. Then I left them to fell the timber. Many trees were cut, limbed and then hauled up to our working area by Dave, who was driving our large B414 tractor. Immediately after the logs were freshly cut, we began stripping off the bark to prepare them for installation into the walls.

We did this work at quite a distance from the building site so there would be no clutter in the area where we would be laying out the concrete foundation for the logs. Since these were foundational logs, they had to be well clear of any soil and moisture; otherwise, they would rot, and if they did, the permanence of the building would be negligible.

Shortly afterward, Herman Martin from Wallenstein and Harry and Muriel Lockhart from Fergus arrived to help for a week. Both of the men were retired farmers and knew what had to be done, sticking to it until it was finished. With their help, we set up the framework of boards where the footings would be. The concrete footings were 24 inches wide and 8 inches deep, and they extended all around the perimeter of the building where the logs would lie. Harry mixed the cement at the machine, Herman wheeled it over to the footings and I levelled and dressed it up, ready for it to set and harden. By the end of that week, we had the footings poured for the complete layout of the building. Now we were ready to begin work with the logs.

OVERRUN WITH WORKERS

The footings which delineated the building gave us an impression of how large it would be. Our plans were to lay up the logs all around the building, one course at time. This would knit the kitchen and ice house to the main dining area via the foyer, which would be between the two. In the foyer area, which was central to the whole building, we had allowed for a furnace room to heat the building in wintertime. We envisioned that a winter camp might be held on the odd occasion; this would make the Camp facility even more useful and enjoyable. We planned for this possibility by making a strong, solid foundation for a stone chimney. The building grew in height as each log was fitted to the one below. Fibreglass insulation was inserted between the logs to make the walls draftproof. This worked out very well.

The first year, we managed to get the logs four high in the dining area and to install several window frames therein. This was in 1972. During that year, Ross Woodward and Norm MacPherson, along with their wives Thelma and Doris, were with us for the latter part of the summer. The two capable women took over the cooking so that Verna could have a break. Ross taught

Bible studies along with Charlie while Norm was very useful in general maintenance.

A new experience: laying logs

The workers who came knew quite well that this was a *faith work*. All the work, and all the expense of their coming was their own responsibility and the Lord's. We fed them while they were here; even that cost was provided by what the Lord sent in by gifts. The funds needed to keep the ministry functioning were provided by Christians as the Lord touched their hearts in sympathy of what was going on. We frequently received checks in the mail for this purpose. This is difficult for some people to understand and believe, but is true. Likewise, machinery and tools that we needed were provided by the Lord, one way or another. For example, as mentioned, we received the logs we needed as a gift. I make this point so we may remind ourselves that what God says in Psalm

50:10–12 is true: "For every beast of the forest is Mine, and the cattle on a thousand hills. I know all the birds of the mountains, and the wild beasts of the field are Mine. If I were hungry, I would not tell you; for the world is Mine, and all its fullness." He speaks here of living creatures, but we may also include all circumstances throughout the world and beyond this planet; all are under His control, and He wants us to come to know Him through his Son Jesus Christ. Everyone needs to understand this!

Another real asset to the effort of establishing the camp was one deserving of honourable mention. Her name is Elsie Pellow. She resided in Chapleau and was a permanent resident there. Elsie received calls from anyone trying to reach the Camp during the summer. She gave necessary directions and answered all inquiries, since back then there was no telephone service at the Camp, as there is now. Elsie's work was invaluable to us at that time, and we assume it still is as the Camp ministry continues to function. Elsie is in fellowship with the Christians who meet at the Community Bible Chapel in Chapleau.

---- CHAPTER 12 ----

The Big Job Continues

SUGGESTIONS MAKE THE JOB EASIER

The following year, the usual letters came in asking if we needed help at specific times in the summer. This help was gratefully received and we started into the log work again. Since this was my first attempt at building with logs, I used a corner design that I thought was practical, even though it was time-consuming to make and crude-looking. When the girls camp was in operation that year and we were coming to the end of the summer, Leo Vezina from Chapleau brought his daughter out for a camping experience. He approached me and cautiously asked, "Did you ever think of using a saddle joint at your corners?" I said, "No, describe it to me." He did, and I saw the wisdom in his suggestion. My job became much, much easier, and much simpler. Thanks, Leo!

In what I have written, I hope that by now, readers have noticed that all along, the Lord came to my rescue with help or advice or even other ways to illustrate that "His yoke is easy, and His burden is light." These experiences also confirmed to me that this work was the Lord's and that we were but His servants. Since it was the Lord's work, there would be no lack of supply in anything we did. The important thing was to maintain a spirit of faith in Him and of love for one another as we laboured together. Underlying currents of ill feeling toward anyone would be devastating to the work since "man looks on the outward appearance, but God looks on the heart" (1 Samuel 16:7). Harbouring ill feeling toward anyone in the Body of Christ breaks our bond of fellowship with one another and with the Lord. As well, the work you are trying to do will come to a standstill. This is especially true in Christian endeavours. "Truly, our fellowship is with the Father, and with His Son Jesus Christ" (1 John 1:3). The next verse assures us that "fullness of joy will follow."

Ron, laying logs

Leo came back at the end of the camping session to pick up his daughter. He asked us how the log laying was doing. "Just great, since your suggestion," I said, "but now I have another problem: When I start the combination welder-generator, it runs, but it will not produce electricity." He replied, "That one is simple. Do you have a car battery handy?" I said that I did and went to fetch it. He explained that the generator had lost its magnetism. All he did to fix it was touch the positive terminal of the generator with the positive terminal of the battery. He started up the generator and, behold, it was working! Thank you, Lord, and thanks for Leo's help.

ENLARGEMENT MAKES FOOD STORAGE BETTER

In the beginning, I realized that we needed to have some way to preserve our food. For the first year or two, we got by with a used kerosene refrigerator, but as the Camp's numbers grew, this became far from adequate. We had to think in larger terms. We had no access to Ontario Hydro because the hydro lines were several miles away from the camp gate in either direction, so electric power for refrigeration was unavailable. Consequently, we had to come up with some way to preserve our food during the summer months. The answer was to build an ice house.

In designing what was to be the log kitchen area, we set aside a space at the end of the building that was 16-foot square. After the logs were laid for the kitchen area, we built a cube-like with measurements of seven by seven by seven feet. This was not made of logs, but ordinary lumber. Within this cubicle, we would store food during the camping season. It would be accessible by a short hallway leading from the back log wall of the kitchen. All around this cubicle, we reserved a four-foot space on each side, and on top, which we would fill with blocks of ice. These blocks could easily be cut from the lake with a chainsaw in January, or when the ice was at its maximum thickness.

An Ice House Preserves Food Better

After the log work was all done on the kitchen area, in early January we organized an ice-cutting bee. This was usually done at the school break in either December or January. The operation didn't begin until we had a good thickness of ice on the lake, usually 20 to 24 inches. The cutting of the ice was done with a chainsaw with an especially long bar, about 24 inches. Then the cut ice was floating freely in the water, and we removed them from the lake by the following means. The blocks were pulled (slid) up a plank and piled uniformly on a large sleigh. This sleigh was provided by Herman Martin. He previously had used it on his farm. Then the sleigh was dragged (an easy job with the tractor) about 300 feet up to the door of the ice house.

We used the bucket on the front of the tractor to lift the blocks of ice up and into the ice house, where an attendant received them. He would fit them into place using a pair of ice tongs. Three or four of us could put up ice quite easily, so it took only one day, two at the most, to complete the job. Then we covered the ice well with sawdust, which was readily obtained from any of the several local sawmills. The sawdust lasted for several years, and the ice would last until mid-August of the following year. From then on, until the camp closed for the summer, we used the electric power produced by our costly gas generators only sparingly, giving preference to the needs of our refrigeration first. This pointed to a need for a larger and cheaper running diesel generator, but we set aside this need until the Lord made it clear we should seriously think about it. Fuel costs were saved by turning off the gasoline- or diesel-driven generator during the night. This practice led to an interesting event during the teens' camp, which was always at the end of August, just before the Camp closed.

George Howard on a load of ice

After the log kitchen and dining area was built and operational with electric lights, the teenagers would gather there in the evenings for food, fun and fellowship, playing games or sitting huddled in some corner just shooting the breeze. However, every night the reverie would be interrupted by that nasty camp director's voice (mine) shouting a warning above the racket: "Lights are going out in 15 minutes!" I gave this warning because

I always shut the generated power off at ten thirty p.m., mainly to preserve operating costs but also to provide quiet during sleeping hours. (Actually, I usually extended the time so that no one would be disappointed.) The girls would immediately run for the door and to their cabins, take up their electric curling irons and reset their hair for the next day. When they did this, you could hear the generator begin to labour and to slow down due to the heavy demand of the hair curlers. Another regular event was when many headed for the toilets to make that last visit prior to lights out. If they weren't among the first to get there, often there was no water for the second flush. This was because when the power was off, there was no water pressure to refill the toilet tanks with more water. If the toilets were not functioning due to the lack of water, the teens would have to visit the outhouse instead, and *in the darkness*. These were humorous daily events before we had sufficient power and funds to keep electricity available all night long.

At the close of the 1972 camping season, we had the main dining area, kitchen area, the foyer and furnace room delineated, with all the logs laid in place, four logs high. By 1973, we were all set to continue the log work and hopefully, to finish it that summer.

Faithful Workers and Givers Make the Work Go On

Murray Martin from Wallenstein Bible Chapel offered to come for a full summer to help me with the log work on the walls. This was in the summer of 1973. By the end of that year, we had built all of the logs up to ceiling height. This included the area of the dining hall and the kitchen. Earlier that year, Martin Tile Yard in Parkhill had said they would provide the steel truss-work for the second floor of the log building. At the beginning of the teens' camp, we received the steel truss from them. Emerson Martin located used trusses in his area and added more structure to them, making them suitable for our needs. These were brought here by one of Jorma Saari's trucks. He made sure they were brought up on a return trip from delivering a load of lumber to Toronto. As mentioned, his business was trucking loads of lumber from Island Lake to wherever they were directed, generally southern Ontario.

Upon the arrival of the truss, the teens' camp was in session. Any young men who were willing workers helped carry them to the inside of the log building, where I could hoist them up with the tractor. At this time, there was only a gravel floor inside, making it difficult to manoeuvre the tractor since it did not have the luxury of power steering. However, we were thankful just to have a tractor to lift the truss. We had built a boom for the front end of in order to lift the trusses high enough to lay them on the walls in their designated place. This was particularly fast and easy with all the ready hands that were there to carry them in and the others up on the wall waiting to anchor them where they were to be placed.

During all of this construction, the scheduled camp sessions carried on to the glory of God. Some might frown to think that construction carried on during the camping season, yet we had no choice. The Lord prospered our work and was glorified through the teachers of the Word of God. At that time, it was Charlie Shorten and Dr. Ross Woodward. Happy were our times working together!

Ross and Thelma, Charlie and Betty

During that summer, Gloria, Emerson Martin's daughter, was with us. Occasionally, Murray Martin and Gloria would go for an evening canoe ride out on the lake. I often wondered what their conversation was all about during those outings. In any case, whether this led to *that*, or that led to *this*, in process of time, Murray and Gloria tied the knot and became Mr. and Mrs. Gladly, we recall that both their fingerprints are all over Wildwood.

I had lifted up the trusses as they were brought in using the front-end loader on the tractor. This hydraulic lift unit, or front-end loader, as it is called, was also a gift from Martin Tile Yard in Parkhill, through our dear brother in Christ, Emerson Martin. Emerson was one of the Martins who had a responsible position at the Martin Tile Yard in Parkhill. Other useful items were sent up as gifts as well, namely several hundred clay tiles to construct our two tile beds in both washrooms, and a large farm windmill to pump water and supply water pressure for the kitchen in the earlier days. All this was searched for, paid for and sent up on one of Jorma's trucks. I do not remember the couple who donated the windmill, but God knows them and will reward them in His own time. All were gifts to the Lord's work and to our benefit, making our work much easier. When the trusses were in place, we were ready to cover it with wood flooring. This pertained only to the dining area in 1973.

When the teens' camp ended, normally the Camp was closed up, but this time, Murray Martin stayed on to help me nail the flooring in place on top of the truss. Shorty Morris was with us as well, and he did what he could to make things easier for us. He became our first-class cook. As well, while Murray and I worked on laying the flooring, he supplied us with items we needed. Those days were satisfying and relaxing. We ate in the evenings by lamplight, talking about and sharing the important things of the Lord together.

A Concrete Floor Preserves the Footings Better

When the upper flooring was all in place, Murray headed home for Wallenstein. One more job remained: Our goal was to get the concrete floor poured in the main log building before frost and winter set in. Herman Martin learned of this and arranged for two young fellows from Wallenstein Bible Chapel to come up with him in September. The plan was that the four of us would put in the concrete floor together. For that event, Bob Hanks, who is now with the Lord, came over from Timmins to make the work easier.

The fellows who came with Herman shovelled the gravel by hand. Bob wheeled all the cement from the two mixers over to us, and Herman and I levelled it out. Every square foot of the floor was trowelled by hand. This took two days to accomplish, but when it was done, the summer's work was over. The Lord had seen us through the summer, and what a joy and blessing it was working with all who were there! Besides that, all the bills were paid up at the end. "Let us with a gladsome mind praise the Lord for he is kind." The roof was not yet on the building, but we were sure it would manage quite well through the winter.

It was totally amazing to me to see how the Lord kept supplying us with materials for the job, whether by direct gift or by the cash needed to buy them, and even with workers voluntarily offering to come and help if we needed them. These occurrences convinced me all the more that this work was of the Lord. Jesus said, "Take My yoke upon you and learn of Me, for I am gentle and lowly in heart, and you will find rest for your souls. For My yoke is easy, and My burden is light" (Matthew 11:29–30).

CHAPTER 13

Incidentals—Part One

WINDOWS AND DOORS JUST FOR THE TAKING

Prior to the erecting of the log building, I was in the centre of Chapleau one day when I noticed something major going on. They were beginning to demolish the local high school. This had been talked about for some time, and now the demolition was underway. It crossed my mind that the windows and doors might be up for sale. These would be quite useful in the Camp's main dining area. I knew they would be of top-notch quality which, if I'd had to buy them, would have been very expensive. I stopped and spoke to one of the officials to ask what was going to happen to them. He replied that the doors and windows were going to the dump. I immediately asked whether I could have some for the new building we were constructing at the Camp.

"How many do you want?" he enquired. "I'll save them for you." I estimated a number, adding a few extra in case of breakages that might occur while dismantling the building. Then the topic of doors arose. "How many do you need?" Once again, I gave him a generous figure and he said," I'll see what I can do.

Just take them out of our road within a few days or they may get damaged."

My reply was a hasty, "Yes, sir!" Sure enough, I got my prize within a few days. This included two sets of double doors, some good single doors and all the windows for the upstairs. There were also some large pieces of slate which could be used as old-fashioned chalkboards in teaching sessions at the Camp.

Scripture once again came to mind: "Being on the way, the Lord led me" (Genesis 24:27). The sizes of the doors and windows we got from the old high school determined the sizes of the openings for these units in our log building. That was a big load off my mind. The windows for the first level, on which there would be much heat generated by all the people and by the preparation of food, were designed to be sliders that could open easily if ventilation were needed. Jim Demers offered to build these for us when we were ready. He did, and they bore the stamp of a master craftsman!

HOT WATER ALWAYS AVAILABLE

The kitchen was progressing and would soon be ready. Now we needed some means of heating water for doing dishes and cleaning up. This could be done using propane, which would be less work but more costly. We could consider it later on, but for now, we were interested in minimizing expenses. We opted for a wood-burning unit outside the building, and built no higher than the level of the ground. Water could circulate through a series of pipes inside the dome of a large firebox. Since hot water rises and cold water falls, this would create a natural circulation and hot water would store itself in a tank above the ceiling of the kitchen. This system would work quite well when it was ready. Every way we could save operations costs helped to keep camping fees down. The next thing we needed was a large tank in which to store the hot water. This was provided by Martin Tile Yard again, when they heard of our need.

During the winter months, Alec would periodically appear as usual and would ask what was going on at the Camp. Occasionally, we would go out there for three or four days and work on putting insulation and a false ceiling in the cabins, especially the staff cabins, so that some of them would be more comfortable in the summer months. To get into the Camp, we would have to plough and sometimes shovel our way through snow in order to get close to the cabins inside which we wanted to work. Soon other people heard of our work there in the winter.

Snow blower in good use

Herman Martin had been to the campgrounds on many occasions, and he was anxious to see the project move ahead according to plan, so he located for us a snow blower that would fit on the back of the tractor. This enabled us to get in during winter with ease. He and Minerva brought it north to us on a surprise visit. It proved to be a real asset for getting jobs done during winter.

STRENGTH FOR THE INNER MAN

When the day's work was done during those winter visits, darkness would settle in. Since we had no electricity, we would relax for the evening by lamplight. It was too cold to start a gas engine for electricity, so we did what we could without any power. Alec would reach into his suitcase and extract a book he had brought along so that we could enjoy it together. Usually, the book was about the deeper things of the Christian life. This, of course, would be after supper, once we'd satisfied the physical needs of our bodies and the dishes were done. Then it was time to feed the spiritual man. This would carry on until we were yawning often, indicating it was time to stoke the fire, blow out the light and crawl into bed.

A NIGHT TO REMEMBER

In following the narrative of how we established Wildwood Bible Camp, readers may be thinking, *God led you and blessed you so much that there must have been times when Satan was working against you.* Yes, definitely yes. These situations usually concerned doubts on my part about whether I was going in the right direction with certain decisions. Generally, I would pray about the direction I had taken until I had peace from the Lord that it was the right way. Then I would move forward or change my direction accordingly. However, there was one special night that I shall not forget for some time. I am a bit reluctant to mention this, but it was an important event and one that illustrates the power in the name of the Lord Jesus.

The occasion was similar to what I described above: Alec and I were retiring for the night. Alec slept in a bed and I in a bunk. Having gone to bed for the night, all that we could hear was the crackling of the wood burning in the stove. I soon drifted off and was fast asleep, as per usual. About two hours had passed when I was awakened by Alec getting up and stoking the fire. The fire usually lasted about two hours because it was shut down with its drafts closed for the night. After adding more fuel, he closed the lid, and then, feeling the call of nature, he stepped outside to relieve himself. A moment later, I heard him return and crawl into bed.

Suddenly, I felt a pressure on the edge of my mattress. It felt like something weighing about 30 pounds. Then, the weight shifted, a bit at a time, and started moving, about 10 inches at a time. I thought at first it was Alec playing some sort of a joke on me, yet I knew that that was not in his character; he would not disturb anyone who was asleep in bed with a practical joke. The movement shifted past my feet and up the other side of my body, eventually coming up to my head. I sensed that this was the power of darkness and tried to speak. With difficulty, I uttered, "Jesus is my Lord, Jesus is my Lord." However, it was as if my voice and ability to speak were paralyzed, for this was very difficult. The dreadful experience passed in a couple of minutes, and I was able at least to whisper again, "Jesus is Lord." I wondered whether I had been dreaming. To check if this were so, I spoke to Alec.

"Alec," I said.

"Yeah."

"Did you just stoke the fire?"

"Yeah," he replied.

"Did you just go outside to relieve yourself?"

"Yeah, Why?"

"I just had the strangest experience. I'll tell you about it in the morning."

This confirmed in my mind that the event had been real and I had not been dreaming. I was glad it was over.

Many people do not understand that there are unseen spiritual powers controlling, or wanting to control human beings. We are subject to them unless we belong to Jesus Christ. These powers of darkness either try to hinder, or to stop completely works of God. I believe this is what was happening in my case. I was well aware that the Camp we were bringing into existence was a place where the Gospels would be preached and where lost souls would be saved from a life of ungodliness and restored to God by faith in the Lord Jesus Christ. Everything we were doing was for the glory of God. He is glorified when sinners repent of their sins and trust in Jesus as Saviour and Lord. This trusting in Christ delivers them from the judgment of God and releases them from the slavery and power of Satan in their lives, setting them free.

The devil hates this salvation and also those who propagate it. This is because an individual who trusts Christ is delivered from Satan's control and slavery. He is given a new life in Christ and a life of power to live righteously, which is God's desire for him. The believer must acknowledge Christ as his Lord in order to confirm this (see Luke 10:17–20); it delivers the believer from the authority of Satan. The Word of God declares that the believer in Christ is seated with Him in the heavenly places in Christ Jesus (Ephesians 2:6–7) and far above all principality and power and might and dominion (Ephesians 1:21). When a believer understands this and claims this position in Christ, it sets Him free from the power of darkness. This is why I claimed that Jesus Christ is my Lord. I am no longer under the authority of Satan as I was before I believed in Christ. This declaration that "Jesus is Lord" is what set me free from the attack I was experiencing at that moment. These powers of which I write truly exist. We must choose this day *whom* we will serve!

When morning came, I told Alec the whole story. He replied with only one word: "Humph." To Alec, it didn't seem like much, but to me, it had been very real. I don't know what I could have experienced besides the forces of darkness. When a work of the Lord by faith, such as the establishing of Wildwood Bible Camp, is going on, it is very unusual *not* to have some sort of spiritual warfare present as well. Up to this point, all materials that we needed were there or were on their way; this convinced me that the work was of God. These forces had no way of gaining victory over me because I had identified their presence and taken my stand by claiming Jesus Christ is Lord (see Philippians 22:8–11). "And being found in fashion as a man, He humbled Himself and became obedient unto death, even the death of the cross. Therefore, God also has highly exalted Him and given Him the name which is above every name, that at the name of Jesus every knee should bow, of those in heaven, and of those on earth, and of those under the earth, and that every tongue should confess that Jesus Christ is Lord, to the glory of God the Father." This was the ground I stood upon, knowing that by faith, I was seated with Christ in the heavenly places with Him and was in the place of victory over these forces. By stating that "Jesus is Lord" (Ephesians 2:4–10) I had deliverance from them. I will not say that there were not rocky times in the future years in regards to other believers, but these things are in the hands of the Lord, and He will settle things in His own time.

Useful Tools to Make Things Easier

Herman Martin had the camp much on his heart. He was a farmer near the Wallenstein area and close to retirement. He was constantly a great help in the effort. It was also Herman who found a bell for the Camp. We placed it just outside of the main doors so that the kitchen staff could call the campers when meals were ready. Knowing who had obtained the bell for us, we had nicknamed it "Herman's Holler." It reminded all within earshot, "It is time to eat!" This is just the beginning of the list of gifts and efforts Herman gave to the camp. He built a trailer and a rack for carrying canoes for the campers' overnight canoe trips. He gave us a large farm sleigh for bringing in ice to store for summer and also a farm wagon. Being on the Board of Directors, he took a real interest in the Camp. Perhaps I should not mention all these things, since he did it all unto the Lord and the promotion of the Gospels, but these were all such useful items to us.

One day, Herman said to me, "I see you are putting up a lot of buildings here. Does the camp authority own the property?" I shared with him that we had a 21-year lease on the property, but could buy it for $3500. However, since all the monies received thus far had gone into development, we had not done anything about buying it yet. Herman offered to loan the Camp the money, interest-free, for five years so that we could buy it. This proposal was brought before the Board of Directors and was agreed upon by all. We received the loan from Herman and paid for the property in full. It was not long before the money was paid back to him in full and the property was free of any debts.

---- CHAPTER 14 ----

Enclosing the Log Building

A Hive of Activity

The summer of 1974 was upon us. Staff were lined up for the summer, as well as others who could give some time to help us get the second level of the log building erected. We already had the second floor installed; it overhung the lower building by 24 inches all around. This would make it appear like a larger building sitting on top of a smaller one. Proportion-wise, it would still have a pleasing effect to the eye.

The plan was to erect the second level with vertical logs and make the entire second storey eight feet high. We would need several strong young men to help cut the poles, peel, shape and prepare them for vertical assembly. Each pole would have 50 percent of the log cut off at the bottom 12 inches to allow it to sit on the edge of the floor. The poles would extend down below the level of the floor by 12 inches, giving them a firm foundation on which to sit. In this way, they would also hide the floor joists and steel truss all around the building. Once in place, they would be nailed securely.

The vertical poles would be grooved on each side with a chainsaw so they could receive a tongue of quarter-inch plywood. This would make the building windproof and weatherproof. Steel mesh would be secured over the plywood tongue on the inside in the future, so that the surface could be plastered with mortar. The top of the line of poles on the walls would be held uniformly in place with a two by six plank, making them one solid unit. This would be firmly nailed. In this manner, the walls could be soon assembled and braced temporarily. This would hold them in place in readiness for the roof truss that would soon follow. The windows would be placed in the walls using dimensions that would make them look aesthetically pleasing.

A Main Attraction: The Stone Chimney

Many heard of the work we were doing and various artisans expressed a wish to join us. While the upper wall was being built, Cecil Bauman and Arnold Spears were erecting the stone fireplace and chimney at the lower level. Cecil was quite proficient at the job because this was the work that he did in southern Ontario. By the time the upper external walls were in place, the stone chimney was at the level of the second floor. At that time, Cecil had to leave; Arnold carried on through to the roof level and right up to the chimney cap by himself. This included the work on the surface of the upper fireplace, as well as the hearth. These fireplaces display excellent workmanship and really enhance the log work simply by their presence.

While Arnold carried on with his work, we constructed the trusses for the roof. This was accomplished on the floor of the second level while we had a clear area on which to build them. Then we were ready to start the roof structure to close in the building. When the roof was ready, there was lots of help available to hoist it up into place. It was not long before the shape of the roof became apparent. Within a few days, the gable ends were closed in with their vertical logs, and the fascia board enclosed the ends of the rafters. Next we could apply the roof sheathing and lay the asphalt shingles in place. These were nailed mostly by Gord Weber and Eric Freide. At last, the building was closed in from the weather.

When the roof lumber was being installed, Arnold's work on the chimney was at a height that enabled him to work right from the roof. As he needed certain stones to work at the higher level, it was necessary to hoist them up in a bucket by means of a rope within a pulley. Upon completion of the stonework, he then formed the chimney cap and poured it with cement. And then his job was finished. It just remained for the masonry to cure before any heat was sent up the chimney.

Within the chimney there were four flues: one for the upper fireplace; another for the lower fireplace; another for the furnace, which was close to the chimney in its own room; and the last to accommodate the smoke of the Dutch oven. The Dutch oven would be used for baking bread. While waiting for the dough to rise, cooks would stoke a fire in the Dutch oven and allow it to burn for some time. Then it would be cleared of ashes and the bread put inside to bake. Today the chimney stands as a masterpiece built by capable men with artistic ability.

The Lord, Our Unfailing Provider

As news of the camp and our financial policies spread from person to person, so did the increase of potential supplies and donations.

Again, we were seeing, understanding and experiencing the wonderful truth as expressed by Hudson Taylor of the China Inland Mission: "God's work done in God's way will never lack God's supply."

I am sure readers have been able to see that enough materials and even finances, which I have hardly mentioned, were offered so that the work could continue without interruption throughout the summer months. Our needs would present themselves and then the very thing needed would be supplied. The need of some piece of equipment would cross our minds and then that equipment would be in our hands at an unimaginably low cost. I could mention the two tractors, the five-ton truck, the first electric generator and the second. Then there were all of the logs we needed for the log building, complete kitchen furnishings and fixtures and structured steel gussets to support the outer edges of the overhanging truss. Transportation of the major items was provided by Jorma Saari at no cost to us. A large supply of nearly new spring mattresses for the campers' beds was donated to us. In the early days, when the campers' cabins were being built, Alec Macdonald had remembered that a mining company in the Sudbury area had closed operations at Elliot Lake and he was sure they would have surplus mattresses. He made arrangements to get them to the Camp.

Still, I could go on, or others could. I can say unequivocally that God has been in control in supplying the bulk of the needs of the Camp, if not in tangible gifts, then in donated labour or financial gifts. This is not to mention His care of the workers and campers over the years; there have been no serious accidents on the grounds or at the waterfront. As I recall these memorable facts, Verna and I feel extremely blessed to have been part of it all and to have come to know our Lord God in a deeper way and to learn how He works.

"Without faith it is impossible to please God, for He that cometh to Him must believe that He is, and that He is a rewarder of those who diligently seek Him" (Hebrews 11:6).

Finally, the Ladies' Big Moving Day

Finally, the roof truss covering the foyer, furnace room, kitchen, ladies lounge and ice house was constructed and then hoisted in place mainly by manpower. Once this was sheathed over with lumber and shingles were put in place, that area was protected from the weather. This allowed the ladies to bring some of the equipment and kitchen necessities over to the new work area.

During our first summer running the girls' camps, Susan Dickson of Mississauga, Ontario, was that program's Director. She had stayed with us during a previous summer, running a DVBS experience for children in our area. This was how we first met her and her parents, Ken and Marg. At that time, Wildwood Bible Camp had only been in the thinking stage. When we were constructing the log building, I heard from Ken. He was in the restaurant business and he was wondering whether we could use any used restaurant equipment for the Camp's kitchen area. I responded gratefully in the affirmative and breathed a thank you to the Lord, who was right on schedule in supplying the kitchen appliances we needed. These included some stainless-steel work counters, as well as one of bonded wood, some sinks and various other pieces of useful equipment such as a large gas stove. These were excess pieces in Ken's business, and they were ours just for picking them up. This involved a trip to Toronto and back again. Jorma's trucks helped us out, as usual, on several occasions and under his direction. He would instruct one of his drivers to backhaul large articles too big for us to handle ourselves. Usually, after the trucks had delivered their loads of lumber, they came back empty, so Jorma was glad to backhaul our items from Toronto to the Camp.

When I mentioned that there were kitchen furnishings available, Jorma wanted to backhaul them personally, instead of sending one of his drivers. I went along with him, and we slept on the load of lumber that night in the heart of Toronto. Listening to the noises of the big city through the night, we both agreed that we would take the bush any time! He dropped off his load and then picked up the furnishings for the Camp's kitchen at the Dicksons'.

The dream accomplished

On one occasion, Verna and I were in Cambridge, Ontario; I was speaking at the assembly where the late Robert McClurkin had been prominent. We had the pleasure of staying overnight with Robert's widowed wife. She had made arrangements to give us a large matching set of dishes which they used during conferences; she wanted the Camp to have them. That was many years ago; I wonder whether they are still being used.

Summer was drawing to a close. To crown the summer's work, the ladies continued moving the furnishings of the old kitchen into the new one. Meanwhile, I was busy constructing the log stairway up to the second floor. This was all chainsaw work to keep the logs concept in harmony throughout the building. Having the stairs in place enhanced the speed of the work being carried out upstairs, including the installation of the school windows, wiring for lighting, insulation and covering the ceiling with plywood. Alan Poyntz worked at plastering the joints of the vertical logs on the second floor while his wife Joan directed the girls' camp.

Strength for the Truss and Heat for the Building

With the upper storey of the log building pretty much in place and the steel truss extending beyond the lower walls, I feared that the weight of the walls of the upper structure might prove too great for the truss, especially when the load of the winter's snow fell upon them. Who could know how heavy the snowfall would be in a severe winter?

This led us to consider the need for triangular-shaped steel gussets that would be welded to each truss, thus transferring the weight of the upper wall to the side of the log wall below. These gussets were manufactured to size and provided for us by Onias Weber, who had a steel-fabricating business in the Hawksville area.

This man was the grandfather of Owen and Nelson Weber. Owen visited often; he was the one who suggested the need for such gussets. However, it did not stop there. Onias was responsible for the building of the wood-burning furnace and the provision of the same. He also did his work as unto the Lord. At times, the furnace has been fired up to heat the main log building during winter activities. This was cozy indeed. On one occasion, Onias came to see the log building and how and where his work was being used. It was a pleasure to have him there.

CHAPTER 15

The New Is Always Appreciated

A NEW TABLE SAW

One day, we had surprise visitors at the camp. They were a Christian couple from Rockwood, near Guelph, where I had been teaching before the Lord called us back to Chapleau and the Camp. We were well-acquainted with them in connection with the local school board and the Christian community in the area. Their names were Alan and Helen Macdonald. Alan was a design engineer at Rockwell in Guelph, where he designed table saws and other required articles for the company to build.

He had received a bonus for his latest creation, which was doing very well on the markets, and so Alan wanted to share the bonus with us in the form of the saw he had designed, the "Rockwell Beaver." He and his wife, Helen, had heard of the work we were doing and personally brought up one of the saws; it was all crated up and ready to assemble. These dear people went beyond the denominational barriers because they understood the sweet fellowship of Christians in the whole Body of Christ. The Lord has blessed us so much in giving us the full concept of the Body of Christ, and also the wisdom to recognize that Christ is its Head. Praise His Name!

How wonderful it is that the Lord moved the hearts of some Christians to bring us just the tool we needed to do a better job, and with pleasure. That was how we felt when we received the Macdonalds' gift. Soon we had the table saw wired up for operation.

New Workers and New Tables

Prior to the end of the camping season, we had a visit from Doug and Morven Barnes and their young son, Nathan. He is a grown man now, but when they arrived at the Camp, he was just a little lad running around. They had arrived in Chapleau with the intention of getting involved in the Camp ministry. In time, Doug was added to the Board. As I recall, we had not long ago finished the major work on the log building. Since that was accomplished, we began thinking about new tables for the dining area. Some time before, I had been thinking of an appropriate design, something that would be simple to build. The tables currently in the dining area were the result of that concept. I calculated the materials needed and made a trip to Sheppard and Morse, the company that dealt in white pine. We were familiar with the place since our first introduction to northern Ontario was when I was working as a schoolteacher there. I made a deal for what we needed and trucked it home to my workshop in Chapleau. There, Doug and I cut up the pieces and assembled them along with matching seat benches. We took these to the dining hall at Wildwood when they were finished and varnished.

Dining room tables

NEW WHEELS AND NEW LIGHTS

Following this effort, Dr. Ross Woodward and Norm MacPherson took on the effort of supplying and installing the beautiful ceiling fixtures. I believe there were eleven in number. They are unique, constructed of wooden wagon wheels, with a number of electric lights placed around wheel and a genuine glass lamp chimney. The closed-in finished ceiling was installed before the ceiling fixtures went up. Once completed, they blended in perfectly with the décor of the logs.

If one strolls through the second level of the building after mounting the log stairway, one enters a large meeting area with a stone fireplace. This constitutes the meeting place in which visiting speakers open the Word of God to nourish the Christians who gather during the family camps. It serves as a place of instruction for boys and girls and teens.

As one leaves the large meeting room, one proceeds centrally down a long hallway with several rooms exiting from either side of the hallway. Some of the rooms are for storage and some are sleeping quarters for the staff or for guests. The hallway exits to a large porch and stairway that communicates to the ground level at the other end of the building. If and when the need may arise, the porch serves as an emergency fire escape. This was constructed by Gord Martin after we had left the Camp. It was a good addition for making the upstairs safe, providing a suitable exit in the event of a fire and also a convenient exit for the building.

New Washrooms for the Cabin Line

Along with the need for the log building and its larger dining facility was a need for more washroom facilities on the far cabin line. Previously, a large area had been cleared of brush with this goal in mind. I made preparations for the underground plumbing that would deliver the effluent from several toilets and lavatory basins. The building was in two sections, with the boys on one side and the girls and ladies on the other; each section had a doorway at the end where the toilets were. At the other end of each section were the washing-up sinks. At this latter end, I allowed for a doorway to connect the sections together. I kept in mind that during the boys' camps, both sides would be used by boys, so the dividing door would be left open. Likewise with the girls' camps. Otherwise, the dividing door would be locked.

For doing laundry, a facility with its own entrance was needed, as was a hot water tank. This was easily provided across the front end of the building, separate from the previously described washrooms.

Prior to laying the concrete floor, all of this underground plumbing had to be installed. When it was ready, the framing and partitions were added according to plan. Shortly after, the fixtures were in place and the building was ready for use by all. This changed much of the general atmosphere and made the camp more of a desirable place for all concerned. These new washrooms and toilets necessitated the building of a large concrete septic tank and a weeping tile bed consisting of clay tiles. Again, these were gifted to us by Martin Tile Yard in Parkhill, Ontario.

CHAPTER 16

Incidentals—Part Two

Our Building Materials

The reader must be curious by now about the Lord's supply of all the lumber we were using. Where did it come from? How was it paid for? Before we go into that question, let's go back to when I was building my own house, shortly before we started building the Camp. I was buying lumber for my house from Chapleau Lumber. This was a sawmill that produced dressed lumber and shipped it to retailers in larger cities such as Toronto.

At Chapleau Lumber, I selected what grade of lumber I wanted and then made the deal, usually for wholesale prices since I was a local resident. From experience, I knew the strengths of different pieces of lumber. For instance, a two-by-four has four sides and four corners. If it is consistent throughout its whole length, it constitutes a top-grade piece of lumber. But if it has, for example, one corner slightly rounded with some tree bark on its full length or part of it, then it will be cheaper in price because it is not as saleable, though just as useful and strong, as a top-grade piece of lumber. At Chapleau Lumber, this was called "back tally." It was usually burned up in a large steel incinerator built for this purpose. Since it was a third or a half off the regular price, I always bought back tally. I got to know the superintendent quite well, and when he learned what I was using all the lumber for, he would sometimes even give me a full five-ton truckload at no charge. Some of it would be scrap, but most of it was useable. In addition to two-inch lumber was some one-inch material that we could use for sheathing. Thus, the Camp's construction kept moving ahead with all bills paid and quality construction.

I became good friends with the main sales manager at Chapleau Lumber. He often wondered how we were doing on our building projects. One time, he mentioned that he had a personal holiday campsite not far from ours. He and his family often wanted to go up there, but they were not able because it was snowed-in during winter. I offered to go over there and blow out the snow on the roadway so they could fulfill their desire for a family holiday. One of their French-Canadian customs was to have a maple-taffy pulling event, which was made possible by the snow and freezing temperature of winter. The children especially enjoyed this. I made it possible for them to get into their property by opening the road, at no cost to them. As you can imagine, this made for a good relationships in buying lumber at cheaper prices.

OUR BIG EVENT

Near the end of the teens' camp, I announced that we had a big event coming up: a midnight hike. Excitement was high as the event drew near. Not until the day of the hike did I announce where we would be going. We would go east on the highway to the power-line trail, then we would follow the power line for about a mile. Our objective would be to see the wildlife at night. We instructed the campers to bring flashlights and to wear more worn clothing because of the roughness of the trail. Special warning was also given that we might see strange people along the way. If anyone felt too chicken to hike and would rather stay back at the camp, he or she was free to do so.

The midnight hike was a lot of fun. Spirits were high as the teens looked for nocturnal animals and stayed on the lookout for the strange people of whom they had been warned. They used their flashlights actively to peer into dark holes and to look for any flying objects that might alight in their hair. Afterward, some of them declared that they had seen the figure of a strange woman with long, curly brown hair. She hadn't bothered them, so they had stayed away from her while wondering what she had been doing back there at that time of night. They didn't realize the Camp Director had been up to some mischief that night.

The midnight hike was the topic of conversation for a long time. To some, it had been an event full of suspense. To others, it had been something to endure. And to yet others, it was the highlight of the week. Many told of how wet their shoes had gotten and how they had tripped and fallen in the mud. "We had a ball!" It's amazing the strange things that entertain young people!

CHAPTER 17

A Necessary Co-worker

THE SPIRIT OF WILDWOOD

I considered my wife to be the spirit of Wildwood. This does not in any way cast an affront on the Spirit of God, who was constantly guiding us in all that we did. What I mean is that the activity of the Spirit of God was in union with Verna's spirit.

Whenever any visitors came, whether they be parents wishing to register their children for the boys' or girls' camps, or anyone else calling unexpectedly, she always offered them a cup of coffee or tea or made some other expression of hospitality. This was an expression of love to all, because hospitality was one of the gifts that God gave her as a Christian. She wanted to reach the people personally and to share the Gospel with them.

Just considering the many meals she prepared for the workers who first built the Camp and all the ongoing daily meals when the camps were in session, she was more valuable than any of us. In some cases, she fed 75 to 90 people each meal, three times a day.

During the off-season, Alec and I sometimes went out to work at the Camp for a few days. She was certainly a major part of that work because she would cook us a tasty stew that we could heat up quickly and eat before getting back to work. All of this was done with a spirit of dedication to doing her part to make Wildwood what it is. Someone has said that marriages are made in heaven. Perhaps this was the case for us.

I mention these events to stress that God has His perfect plan for us and for the sort of helpmeet we will need. I can do mechanical things and perhaps explain some Scriptural doctrine, but it takes a special person to be able to make other people feel welcome and comfortable. By giving them such a good introduction to Wildwood, Verna, presented the ministry of the Word of God, illustrating that it works in the hearts of those who believe. The magnetism of the love of God has a marvellous effect on people's hearts, especially if they have been used to heartache and bitterness. During our married life, Verna and I had two children, Susan and Stephen. We also came to care for two sisters, Lyn and Mary Lucas.

The Millson family

When we hear of the knowledge of Jesus Christ and God's plan that we should be and can be like Him, our hearts and minds are turned to the direction from where we can hear more. This is why places like Wildwood, where folks can come and get acquainted with others, are so necessary. Even people who have already heard of God's plan have yet to find the answers to life in the knowledge of our Lord and Saviour, Jesus Christ. My dear wife has been the complement of my own heart and aims in bringing this place into being so that this goal may be accomplished. Since we have stopped having an active part in this ministry, we have met several people who spoke very positively of the effect Wildwood has had on their lives. Our hearts have been warmed knowing that we had a small part in bringing this Camp into being. Again, maybe marriages *are* made in heaven!

Verna and her kitchen friends

If it were not for Verna's presence in my life as a good and faithful wife to me and a mother to our children, Wildwood Bible Camp may never have come into existence. I have stressed the fact that she was unequivocally the spirit of Wildwood while we were there. Her heart and mind were at the centre of all that was going on at the Camp. As the camp cook, Verna was often visited by the campers, who enjoyed her company. In the photo below, Verna and our daughter Susan are in the centre, Bruce and Diane Reid on Verna's left and a happy camper on Verna's right left.

The theme of this narrative, as readers will have noted, is that *God has no blind alleys*; it also became the title of the book. There was a time that Wildwood might never have become reality because the whole idea seemed like a blind alley. We were one single family facing a big project with no help or financial resources to accomplish the goal. However, a renewal of faith and purpose took place because we knew that God is Sovereign in all things. Then we became convinced that our efforts at Wildwood would not be in vain. It was God's positive will that the Camp be brought into being. We felt personally honoured to be a part of this and were convinced that He would see us through any trials if we but let Him lead us. The vision was renewed and carried out as has been recorded.

CHAPTER 18

Scary Occasions of Fire

WHEN THE SAUNA BURNED TO THE GROUND

We had not been to visit Wildwood for a long time, so Verna and I stopped by toward the end of the summer in 2011. As we walked over the grounds to see what improvements had been made since our last visit, a friend of ours told us of a serious fire they had had that year. Apparently, a counsellor who had not been instructed in the proper care of the sauna, namely that it needs constant supervision while lit, had not kept his eye on things. The sauna had overheated, a fire began in the ceiling and it was not long before the whole building was engulfed in flames. This was during the teens' camp, so a large number of strong, able-bodied young men had been present. Seeing the predicament, they formed a bucket brigade to bring water from the lake and douse the flames. It was too late to save the building, but the real hazard was avoided: many of the trees nearby were cedars, which ignite easily. As I looked at the few trees that had been scorched, I could see it must have been a tense few moments before they'd gotten things under control.

However, the fire had been put out, and there was a good carpenter on the grounds at the time. He rebuilt the new sauna to be identical to the original.

WHEN SMOKE CAME FROM THE LOG BUILDING

After the log building had been finished and was showing its potential as a part of the Camp, it was time for us to rest a little. Summer was at its end and the teens' camp was over. In the mid-morning, the bus left, loaded with its teenaged passengers, headed for southern Ontario, where the year's Wildwood experience would be but a memory. Once the campers were gone, the quiet and stillness of the grounds was almost haunting. Those of us left had different reactions. Verna was still going, concentrating on doing a quick laundry load. She visited each cabin and scanned the grounds to see if any clothing had been left behind—a usual occurrence. Anything found in good condition was laundered and would be taken south on one of our routine trips for the owner to identify. What Steve and Susan were doing, I was not sure. I, however, was horizontal, enjoying my afternoon nap.

For some reason I woke up at about 1:30 p.m. I felt fairly rested, so I decided to get up and begin collecting our things in preparation to close the camp and to leave for home. It was a sunny afternoon. As I left the cabin, heading toward where Verna would be working, I glanced over at the log building. It was something we were rather proud of, now that it was useable. Suddenly, I became startled. As I looked at the roof structure, I could see smoke billowing out from under the eaves of the roof, and it seemed to be increasing in volume. Something was on fire in the building. It must be in the attic.

I ran as fast as I could for the main doors at the side, near the stairs. I flung open the doors and darted upstairs. There I was confronted by a roaring fire in the fireplace. The flames were licking out at the front of the chimney face and upward from the opening about 12 inches. Immediately, I could see what was causing the smoke; it was mainly my fault. Since the surrounding walls were made of vertical logs, I had thought it would be nice to have the face of the fireplace covered with slabs of the same wood, to suit the décor. However, the fire was now licking out beyond the face of the chimney and eating away at the wooden slabs. This was something I had not considered when I put them there. How foolish I had been not to foresee the problem!

As quickly as I could, I took hold of the burning pieces, yanked them from the face of the chimney, ran over to the large window and threw them outside and down to the ground. I was able to get them all off before any serious damage was done. Then I checked the attic and found no problem up there, so I was satisfied that the smoke I had seen had all come from the burning pieces on the front of the chimney. Who knows what might have been if I hadn't woken when I did. I stopped in my tracks and confessed to the Lord my foolishness for not thinking through the possibilities of a fire. Also, I praised Him for waking me when He did so that I could prevent what might have been a disaster.

But with the gang all having left several hours ago, who could have lit the fire and left it burning? It turned out to have been Susan. She was only 14, and already lonely for all of the younger campers she might not see again for another year. She had built a good big fire and reminisced for a while in front of it. Then, not realizing that the face pieces were getting hot enough to burn, she had left the room.

WHEN WE BURNED THE BRUSH AT THE GATE

Doug Barnes had recently moved with his family to Chapleau to be a part of the Camp ministry. One day, he and I went up there to clear some brush at the entrance of the property. After our work was done, we doused the fires. Satisfied they were all safely out, we then left. I believe it was two days later that we came back out to work on something else. While there, we were visited by an officer of Lands and Forests. Apparently, a high wind had come up in the night after we had been burning the brush. Although we had thought the fire was thoroughly doused with water, there were still some embers down below the ash that the wind was able to stir to life again. In the night, these embers had spread to the surrounding area of brush, and a serious fire had started. Thankfully, it was spotted by the government watch towers. They alerted the Chapleau officers, who extinguished it. Doug and I were fined $50 each—a pittance, really, for what it had cost them to extinguish the fire!

WHEN WE REPAIRED OUR SOURCE OF ELECTRICITY

Before we erected a permanent building to house our main electrical generator, the unit became difficult to start. The engine which drove the alternator needed attention. Camp activities were over for the year, and we had time to repair our only source of electricity. The first snow had fallen. Prior to leaving the camp for the winter, we dragged the unit into our workshop to get it under cover and out of the weather. I discovered that the problem was the generator's supply of gas was not getting to the fuel pump. There was a little push rod about four inches long that extended from the engine and connected with the fuel pump. This rod moved back and forth, working the gas pump to move gas to the carburetor. Due to use over the years, the rod had become about an eighth of an inch shorter, and could not now activate the pump. Consequently, I took the rod away to get it lengthened.

One day, Alec appeared at our house and as usual. "What are you doing at the Camp?" he asked. I told him about lengthening the push rod and that it was now ready to install in the engine. He replied, "Well, let's take it out and put it in." This was about 9:00 a.m. We soon got ready and went to the Camp. Milton, our neighbour whom I previously described, made his way over to see what was going on when our truck pulled into the gateway. He talked about various things of interest and watched our proceedings. It didn't take long to reinstall the rod into the unit. Everything was back together except for connecting the battery and the cables.

The gasoline tank containing fuel for the engine was located directly above the unit. This was part of its design. As you might know, over the years, older machines gradually accumulate grease on their sides from dust mixed with gasoline. Such was the case with this engine, and I had neglected to clean it off. As I was putting the cables back onto the battery, there was a spark. It ignited the flammable grease on the sides of the engine block. The flames almost immediately spread to the whole engine, and we realized that the gas tank above might explode over the heat of the open flames. Who could imagine how serious the consequences would be?

Two things happened. First, Alec ran as fast as he could to get the truck and a chain that always lay in the box of the back end. He was soon backing it up to the burning unit and connecting the chain to yank the unit out of the building. The garage door was wide open, which meant that it was lying flat directly above the burning engine. This was a blessing since it shielded the rafters from catching fire.

While Alec was getting the truck, my mind was spinning, set between two choices: Should I wait until Alec moved the unit outside with the truck? If I did, there was a danger the gas tank would explode before we got it outside. Or should I remove the lid of the gas tank now and ignite the fumes to let them burn off? This would lessen the danger of pressure buildup and explosion. I chose the second option, not hazarding a guess as to what may happen in the process of taking off the gas tank lid. This proved to be divine guidance, because, I removed the lid, all was still, I promptly lit a match and ignited the fumes, which burned off without further incident (phew!).

The second thing that happened was rather humorous, to say the least. Milton, expecting a fire or an explosion, ran out of the driveway and headed for the highway and home. As I mentioned, he had a peculiar way of walking on the balls of his feet, half leaning forward. You can image how he appeared when he ran in this posture. He was gone with the wind, so to speak. We didn't see him anymore that day.

After connecting the chain, Alec jumped into the truck, quickly put it in gear and, under the pressure of the imminent danger, popped the clutch to quickly get the burning unit free of the building. The truck lurched forward and out of the shed and clear of the building, the burning engine following. We doused it with snow and eventually, the heat of the moment yielded to the cool of a winter's day.

With things now back to normal, we heard a strange sound coming from the truck engine. It was the sound of running liquid. I lifted the hood to reveal a hole the size and shape of the fan itself now in the radiator. When Alec had popped the clutch, making the truck suddenly lurch ahead, the whole engine had leaned forward on the rubber motor mounts, tearing a hole in the radiator. The running water we heard was the radiator coolant of the truck spilling out onto the ground. Now we were stuck out at the Camp, 24 miles from Chapleau, with no immediate way of getting home!

With the pressure off, reflecting on all the events that had just taken place, including the sight of Milton fleeing, I lay on the hood of the truck and burst into uncontrollable laughter. Added to this was the episode of Alec hastily moving the unit out of the building and free of a major fire on our hands. I could not help but see the humour of our situation. I looked up at Alec, whose look of self-blame told the story of how he felt. I said, "Well, things are not as bad as they could have been. Let's try to figure out some way to get back into Chapleau."

Fire on our source of electricity

Since it would not be needed until a later time, we decided to disconnect the radiator from the gas engine on the unit that drove the alternator. We disconnected the hose cables from the truck radiator, connected them to this radiator and then laid it flat across the top of the truck engine.

We then melted some snow into water and put it in the truck engine, aiming to exchange it for antifreeze as soon as possible. Following more laughter, I said to Alec, "Let's get this rig back to Chapleau!" In this way, we limped our way back home, laughing, with happy spirits. At least we had gotten the little push rod installed in the engine of the electrical unit so it would produce electricity again.

We were thankful to the Lord for leading us out of what we were sure was another blind alley, namely, there being no transportation back home. But there are no blind alleys in God's things—only occasional amusing incidents that add flavourful spice to life. "According to your faith, so be it unto you" (Matthew 9:29).

CONCLUSION

As I draw to a close this account of the beginnings and early operations of Wildwood Bible Camp, I feel compelled to say that the camp has been wonderfully preserved and protected from serious occasions of fire. I believe that the reason for this is that God's watch care has been over the place. I began this memoir in June 2013, and now it comes to completion in April 2014. The writing time has been rather lengthy, but other pressing incidents intervened. However, those incidents gave me more opportunity to remember most of the major events that took place at the Camp. The date that physical activities began at the Camp was May 1969. This means that the Camp had its beginnings 45 ears ago. Uncontrolled fires could have taken over and completely destroyed our efforts over the years, but they haven't. It is only to the safekeeping and care of our loving heavenly Father that we can attribute the fact that the camp has been preserved from fire all this time.

Readers will have noticed that much has been said about the Camp and its establishment being a work of God through His willing servants. This includes men and women, young people and even some children. The Lord has provided physically and financially. In regards to the danger of fires, we admit there have been some close calls. Nevertheless, the Lord's intervention alerted people and moved them into action. Over the years, many people laboured at the Camp during our time there. Unfortunately, their names have not been mentioned. But to them we are sincerely grateful, since without their extra help, the Camp would not have developed as quickly as it did.

Occasionally, we meet children, teens and adults who, when they find out we know of Wildwood, speak about the beauty and restfulness of the place and the pleasant times they have had there. When I mention that we were in it from the beginning, broad smiles come over their faces. Then we have much common ground over which to talk. These folks cherish their fond memories of Wildwood Bible Camp. This speaks well of those who have directed and run the camping programs and of the tasty meals provided by the cooks.

I now turn from my recollections of those early days to speak to you of something very serious. I have been writing of how dreadful and final it is when a fire destroys. Fires are generally used to destroy things that are deemed to have no more value. When we entered this life in infancy, we came as those who were made in the image of God and capable of coming to know Him personally through faith in His Son, the Lord Jesus Christ. He has given all of us a spirit in which the Living God can dwell, but He is unable to do so until we see our need of Him and express our desire for Him. We must recognize that we are all sinners and that judgment lies ahead. We may escape this judgement by desiring to be right with God, by being born again.

If we come to Christ and, in a repentant way, personally believe that He took the punishment for our sins, and if we believe in Him as the Son of God and in His glorious resurrection, then God assures us that we will be born again and given eternal life. In John

3:16, the Bible promises us that we will not perish but receive the gift of eternal life. By this means, we become God's children and need never fear the judgment of God.

However, those, who neglect this wonderful gift will face the final judgment. This is the "Great White Throne" discussed in Revelation 20:11–15. This Bible account tells us that those who are not found written in the "Book of Life" are cast into the "lake of fire." This is God's scrap heap. A scrap heap contains that which was once useful, now has no value. God's judgment upon sinners by nature and by practice is death: "The soul that sins, it shall die" (Ezekiel 18:4). Those who turn their backs on this precious gift of His Son for the forgiveness of sins must depend on their own righteousness—but God has said through the prophets of old that "all our righteousnesses are as filthy rags" (Isaiah 64:6). They are vile in his sight. Such people lack the righteous life that only Christ can give to them. Both the earth and the works that are in it will be burned up, the Bible says. Therefore, "Since all these things will be dissolved, what manner of persons ought you to be in holy conduct, and godliness?" We are advised to be "looking for and hastening the coming of the day of God, because of which the heavens will be dissolved, being on fire, and the elements will melt with fervent heat" (2 Peter 3:11–12). Will you suffer eternally in the lake of fire, or will you be saved from it?

These are serious and sad words to have to write, but they are true words that should make us fear and examine ourselves and accept with, gladness and assurance, this gift of God. I repeat: Our message concerns the Son of God, our Lord and Saviour Jesus Christ, Whom God sent into this world to bear the judgment of our sins. To those who believe in Him and receive Him as personal Saviour, forgiveness is theirs, as is justification in God's sight, as they are made ready to dwell with Him eternally. The Bible also states that "He came to His own, and His own did not receive Him. But as many as received Him, to them He gave the right to become children of God, to those who believe in His name (John 1:11–12). Jesus said, "Come to Me, all you who labour and are heavy laden, and I will give you rest" (Matthew 11:28).

Since our days of founding and administering Wildwood Bible Camp, others have taken over and added many other useful facilities, improving on what was there already. Our continual prayer is that many precious souls will be found in heaven to the glory of God as a result of our labours and theirs.

—Ron Millson